public
spending

ECONOMICS HANDBOOK SERIES

SEYMOUR E. HARRIS, EDITOR

The Board of Advisors

NEIL W. CHAMBERLAIN *Columbia University—Labor*

JOHN M. CULBERTSON *University of Wisconsin—Monetary Theory*

SEYMOUR E. HARRIS *Harvard University—International Economics, Social Security; all other areas*

FRANCO MODIGLIANI *Massachusetts Institute of Technology—Economic Theory*

RICHARD A. MUSGRAVE *Harvard University—Public Policy*

MARC NERLOVE *Yale University—Econometrics and Mathematical Economics*

Burns · Social Security and Public Policy
Carlson · Economic Security in the United States
Duesenberry · Business Cycles and Economic Growth
Fisher · The Identification Problem in Econometrics
Hansen · A Guide to Keynes
Hansen · The American Economy
Hansen · The Dollar and the International Monetary System
Hansen · Economic Issues of the 1960s
Hansen · Monetary Theory and Fiscal Policy
Harrod · The British Economy
Henderson and Quandt · Microeconomic Theory
Hoover · The Location of Economic Activity
Johnston · Statistical Cost Analysis
Kindleberger · Economic Development
Lebergott · Manpower in Economic Growth
McKean · Public Spending
Phelps · Fiscal Neutrality Toward Economic Growth
Quirk and Saposnik · Introduction to General Equilibrium Theory and Welfare Economics
Taylor · A History of Economic Thought
Theil, Boot, and Kloek · Operations Research and Quantitative Economics
Tinbergen and Bos · Mathematical Models of Economic Growth
Vanek · Estimating Foreign Resource Needs for Economic Development
Walton and McKersie · A Behavioral Theory of Labor Negotiations

roland n. mckean

PROFESSOR OF ECONOMICS
UNIVERSITY OF CALIFORNIA,
LOS ANGELES

public
spending

336.39
M154p

mc graw-hill book company

NEW YORK
ST. LOUIS
SAN FRANCISCO
TORONTO
LONDON
SYDNEY

public
spending

Library of Congress Catalog Card Number 67-
19904

45128

2 3 4 5 6 7 8 9 0   MP   7 4 3 2 1 0 6 9 8

to
anne,
meg,
and john

preface

The aim of this book is to help students and other readers understand how public-spending choices are made, what some of the consequences of various choices are, and what would be the effects of using certain instruments to influence those choices. If the book serves its intended purpose, it should help readers decide what policies and actions they prefer. It will not, however, help one decide what policies are correct from a group's standpoint or from the standpoint of the "public interest." For there is no ultimately correct criterion of the public interest. Even if I believe in absolute rather than relative values, and believe that there is a test for these on which people ought to agree, some persons will *not* agree with my values. There is then no demonstrably correct or universally agreed-upon criterion.

To understand how public choices are made, one should look upon individuals—politicians, officials, and voters as well as businessmen and members of households—as utility maximizers. This means that each person gropes for preferredness as *he* sees it; he assesses the costs and gains from alternative actions in terms of his own values and perceptions, for his own senses are the only ones that he can use. Each individual will be attracted toward a mix-

ture of selfish and unselfish objectives. No one gets
up every morning and asks, "What can I do today
to further my conception of the public interest?"
And, as the cost to him of various actions changes,
each individual finds it appropriate to trade a little
of one objective for some of another. This groping,
bargaining, and adaptation among politicians, voters,
and government employees operates like an unseen
hand to constrain each individual and guide decisions.

These basic notions—the functioning of the unseen hand and the lack of an ultimate criterion—
shape the discussion throughout this book, because
they are highly pertinent to the effects of public-
spending policies, to individuals' behavior in deciding what policies they prefer, and to the effects
of using cost-benefit analysis, program budgeting, or
institutional modifications to influence government
action.

The book is not intended as a text. It explores
new territory as well as drawing upon accepted ideas
in order to follow a different approach to the study
of public spending. I hope, however, that the volume will be useful to students in public finance
and administration as well as to economists in general, government personnel, and interested non-
economists.

In connection with writing the book, I owe
many debts of gratitude. The study was begun in
1962 under a grant from the Social Science Research Council to study government processes. More
recently, the Institute of Government and Public
Affairs at the University of California, Los Angeles,
and the Lilly Endowment grant to UCLA made it
possible for me to continue my investigation.
Among the individuals who influenced my thinking,
Armen A. Alchian of UCLA deserves my greatest
thanks. Discussions with him over the last decade
or so have been extremely important to me. I am
indebted in a similar way to James M. Buchanan,
who over the years has contributed much to the

development of my thinking. Special thanks are also due to Messrs. Alchian, Buchanan, and Harold M. Somers for criticizing the entire manuscript, and to Harold Demsetz and Anthony Downs for discussions of particular issues.

I also wish to thank the *American Economic Review* for permission to use portions of my article "The Unseen Hand in Government," which appeared in June, 1965; the *Western Economic Journal* for permission to use passages from an article (with Jora R. Minasian) entitled "On Achieving Pareto Optimality—Regardless of Cost!" (Fall, 1966); Prentice-Hall, Inc., for permission to use passages from my chapter, "Some Remaining Difficulties in Program Budgeting," in *Defense Management*, Stephen Enke, Editor, © 1967; and the International Economic Association for permission to use portions of my paper "Planning and Markets: Modern Trends in Various Economic Systems," presented at a conference held at Nice in September, 1966.

Roland N. McKean

contents

PART 3   some tools for shaping
public choices

part
one

SOME GENERAL CONSIDERATIONS

one

THE SIGNIFICANCE OF PUBLIC EXPENDITURE

Attempts to do *anything* through government entail public expenditure. Even government regulation of private activity, or government effort to gain the cooperation of private groups through persuasion, requires the use of resources—at the minimum, the time of officials or the paper for correspondence. Some of the things that are done may be regarded as good and others as bad. The ancient Egyptians built pyramids, the Romans built roads, Hitler built gas chambers. All these projects entailed public spending. Decisions about government policies and actions are decisions about outlays; and choices about expenditures are decisions concerning policies and actions. This is largely true in private life as well as in government. For that reason, people usually smile when a husband says, "My wife makes all our budgetary decisions, while I take care of the big issues, such as our choices about capitalism, disarmament, and automation."

Public outlays have been powerful tools for shaping societies in the past, and they will have much to do with the kind of world that will confront individuals in the future. To a considerable extent, government budgetary decisions will determine whether the quality of life deteriorates or improves. Some choices can shake nations or even the world—for example, choices about defense posture, the nature of government institutions and the size of government, the transfer and redistribution of wealth, and programs for racial integration. Many other choices, even if they do not yield momentous changes within a few decades, may affect the flavor of life considerably—choices about urban planning, transfer programs, education policies, the manner in which specific programs are conducted, and policies influencing population growth.

Some persons think of the basic procedure as the identification of national goals and the selection of polices to achieve them. This is a perfectly good way to think about the matter as long as one is aware of the implications of thinking in these terms. It may be useful to visualize a little nation consisting of three persons and then to ask: What do national goals mean? If all three persons agree to spend half of their time making a rocket and the other half playing Bach trios, their intentions could be called national goals. If two of the three want to play Bach trios, and the third agrees to abide by the wishes of the majority, the playing of the trios might be labeled the group goal. If the third man says, "Our national goal should be to make a rocket," he is simply trying to persuade the others to accept his preferences. If the three decide to work separately on different things, the agreed-upon goal is to allow each to do as he pleases. Whatever the prevailing decision-making process sanctions might be defined as a national goal. But there is no set of goals that is *inherently* correct for the group—and it does little good to search for such a set.

It is sensible, of course, for each individual to reexamine his own values or preferences, to try to persuade other persons to accept his values, or to try to alter decision-making rules so as to achieve outcomes that he prefers. But it seems useless to look for group aims other than those that individual members agree upon. There is no mysterious, unique set of "correct" group goals that can be identified by thinking deeply or reading the right books or turning over the right rock.

There are many many things, of course, that people *do* agree to work on cooperatively. Often some members of the group dislike what is being done, but they can perceive no *attainable* situation that they would prefer. In any event, people band together to produce shirts, submarines, churches, plays, irrigation projects, and social security programs. Aims to do these things might all be called group goals. People strive for some of these things through nongovernmental organizations. They strive for others through government, and public spending ensues. And, to repeat, the myriad choices involved are extremely important in determining the kind of life that people have.

magnitudes and trends

The significance of public spending can be further suggested by a look at its size and nature in recent years. In the United States, the disbursements of the Federal government were estimated to be about $130 billion for the fiscal year 1966, and state and local outlays were approaching the $100-billion mark. Together, these outlays amount to almost one-third of the U.S. gross national product (GNP). In other parts of the world, public spending also takes a large share of current output. Table 1 indicates the percentages of GNP spent in selected countries by central governments alone (exceptions are noted in the footnotes to the table). Outlays by the central government vary from 7 percent of GNP in Mexico and Nigeria to approximately one-quarter of GNP in Sweden and the United Kingdom. The figures for Poland and the U.S.S.R. are

TABLE 1. Central government expenditures, 1964*
(as percentage of GNP)

	CURRENT TRANSFERS TO HOUSEHOLDS AND LOCAL GOVERNMENTS, %	CURRENT OUTLAYS FOR GOODS AND SERVICES, %	TOTAL EXPENDITURES, %†
Nigeria	1	3	7
Mexico	2	3	7
Japan	7	2	10
India	2	3	13*
Chile	4	7	17
United States	5	10	19
Italy	6	9	20
France	3	10	22
West Germany	7	9	22
Sweden	9	8	24
United Kingdom	10	11	29
U.S.S.R.	—	—	51*
Poland	—	—	55*

* Except for the following: The figures for Nigeria and India are for 1962, and the one for the U.S.S.R. is for 1963. The magnitudes for West Germany are for the central government and the Laender combined. Those for Poland and the U.S.S.R. are for all public authorities combined but presumably exclude state enterprise outlays that are matched by receipts from sales. Also, the figures for India are percentages of **net** national product. And the data are imprecise, especially because of differences in accounting conventions. For these various reasons, the estimates serve one purpose only—to provide clues to the size and significance of these categories of government outlays.
† Includes interest payments, subsidies, public investment, and other disbursements not counted in the first two columns.
Source: United Nations, **Statistical Yearbook 1965**, New York, 1966, pp. 542–553, 597–664.

hard to interpret (see footnotes to table), but, needless to say, the public sector is quite large in those countries.

State and local expenditures are also sizable, varying from one-quarter to
two-thirds of central-government expenditures in most Western nations. With
such outlays included, public spending in the late fifties absorbed 28 percent of
GNP in Italy, 31 percent in West Germany, 32 percent in Austria, 33 percent
in France, and about 40 percent in the United Kingdom.[1]

It is well known that public outlays have grown rapidly during the last century. After World Wars I and II, expenditures did not decline nearly as much
as they had risen during those conflicts.[2] In the United States, Federal outlays
grew from about $3 billion a year in the late twenties to over $125 billion
annually in recent years, and total public spending increased from less than
10 percent of GNP at the turn of the century to almost one-third of GNP nowadays. In the United Kingdom, total government outlays rose from about
10 percent of GNP at the turn of the century to 42 percent of GNP in 1952.[3]
(By 1955 they had slipped back to approximately 37 percent.) Public revenues,
which approximate expenditures, grew in Norway from 10 to 30 percent of
GNP over much the same period. In most nations, the trends have been similar. During the past decade alone, sharp increases in public spending have been
prevalent.[4]

Another significant aspect of public outlays has been the tendency toward
centralization, that is, the shifting of the power of the purse to higher levels of
government. In the United States the Federal share of total government expenditures rose from 35 percent at the beginning of this century to over 60
percent by the early 1960s. The central government in the United Kingdom
spent about 50 percent of all public outlays in 1905 and about 75 percent in
1955.[5] Such changes appear to be widespread, though there is much variability.
By 1957, the central government's share was almost 80 percent in Belgium and
over 80 percent in Italy, France, Greece, and Portugal.[6] (In Switzerland, however, the central government's percentage was only thirty-three.)

The composition of government budgets is also significant. Note in Table 1
that transfer payments to households and local governments form a major com-

---

[1] United Nations, *Economic Survey of Europe in 1959*, Geneva, 1960, chap. V, table
2, p. 8.
[2] *Ibid.*, chap. V, pp. 5–7; Leif Johansen, *Public Economics*, Rand McNally & Company, Chicago, 1965, pp. 153–156; Alan T. Peacock and Jack Wiseman, *The Growth of
Public Expenditures in the United Kingdom*, National Bureau of Economic Research,
Princeton University Press, Princeton, N.J., 1961.
[3] Peacock and Wiseman, *op. cit.*, p. 166.
[4] United Nations, *Statistical Yearbook 1965*, New York, pp. 597–664.
[5] Peacock and Wiseman, *op. cit.*, p. 202.
[6] United Nations, *Economic Survey of Europe in 1959*, chap. V, p. 14.

ponent of public outlays, those by central governments alone ranging from 1 percent of GNP in Nigeria to 10 percent of GNP in the United Kingdom. They are direct transfers and do not include subsidies to stimulate particular outputs or any payments in exchange for services. A breakdown of budgets according to function reveals many striking differences. For example, in 1957 the United Kingdom devoted about 33 percent of total civil-government outlays for goods and services to health, while in Norway only 4 percent was used for that purpose.[7] If one looks at recent outlays of central governments only, one finds that Indonesia put about 1 percent of its central budget into education and another 1 percent into health; Iraq devoted 15 percent to education and 3 percent to health; and Venezuela put 12 percent into each of these areas.[8] Some of the variations occur because countries are in different stages of development and affluence, and their governing officials must respond to different demands. There are many other factors, of course, that lead individual citizens, and leaders, to make diverse choices.

There are also noteworthy differences in the proportions of various functions carried out by different levels of government. For instance, in 1957 Norway's central government allocated 20 percent of its budget to education, while the local governments devoted 45 percent of their outlays to this area. In the United Kingdom in 1957, education received only 1 percent of the central government's expenditures but 54 percent of local outlays. Similarly, Norway's central government spent quite a bit for roads, sewerage, and basic services, matters Great Britain left almost completely to local governments.

Tables 2 and 3 show, in broad categories, the composition of U.S. public spending. The magnitude of defense spending by the Federal government is well known, but to some it may be news that outlays for health and welfare have climbed to an impressive $35 billion. At all levels, but particularly in the state and local governments, the difficulties associated with urbanization may be related to the increasing expenditures for education, highways, health, and housing. In any event, the composition as well as the growth and present size of public expenditures helps indicate their potential significance.

plan of the book

To understand public spending choices that are made and to bring about better decisions, one must examine the way choices are reached by people living in groups. It makes a difference whether policies are selected at random, are chosen according to the whim of one person, are made in accordance with some

[7] Ibid., p. 13.
[8] United Nations, Statistical Yearbook 1965, pp. 597–664.

conception of the public interest, or are decided upon in some other way. The first topic to be considered, therefore, is the "unseen hand in government"

TABLE 2.　　Payments, U.S. federal government, 1966
(in billions of dollars)

National defense	$ 52.6
International affairs and finance	4.0
Space research and technology	5.1
Agriculture and agricultural resources	3.9
Natural resources	2.7
Commerce and transportation	6.5
Health, labor, and welfare	34.8
Housing and community development	0.8
Education	2.7
Veterans benefits and services	5.1
Interest	11.6
General government	2.5
Other (net) adjustments	−4.9
Total	$127.4

Source: **The Budget of the United States Government, Fiscal Year ending June 30, 1966,** p. 16.

(Chapter 2). Since there is no visible controlling hand that plans all government activity, even in authoritarian nations, the forces that shape governmental decisions deserve careful attention.

TABLE 3.　　U.S. state and local expenditures, 1964–1965
(in billions of dollars)

	STATE		LOCAL
	DIRECT	TRANSFER TO LOCALS	DIRECT
Education	$ 6.2	$ 8.4	$22.8
Highways	8.2	1.6	4.0
Welfare	3.0	2.4	3.3
Health	2.7	0.2	2.7
Natural resources	1.2	*	0.5
Housing and urban renewal	*	0.1	1.2
Air transport	*	*	0.4
Interest on debt	0.8	. . . .	1.7
Other	3.9	1.1	12.7
Totals†	$26.1	$14.2	$48.8

* Less than $50 million.
† Because of rounding, the individual amounts do not add to the published totals.
Source: U.S. Bureau of the Census, **Governmental Finances in 1964–1965,** June, 1966, table 6, p. 22.

Next, in Chapter 3 the meanings of efficiency and criteria in public choices will be considered. It has been mentioned that decisions about government spending will exert a crucial influence on the quality of life. Can one determine, then, whether Policy A or Action B will make things better or worse? On the one hand, many persons in the United States feel that life would be improved if the government were to take on additional functions. In other words, they feel that it would be efficient for resources to be used in this fashion rather than in some other way. On the other hand, cynics say that George Washington started things off by throwing a dollar across the Potomac and that the government has been throwing money away ever since. In other words, they feel that too much government spending makes for inefficient use of resources. What is the basis for saying that certain expenditures are efficient or inefficient? Can one insert a piece of litmus paper into a proposal and thereby tell whether or not it is worthwhile? In what sense, if any, is there a test for good or bad policies? It is important to clear up these matters before proceeding further.

Then, in Chapters 4 through 7 we shall take up some major effects or goals of government outlays—redistribution of wealth, reallocation of resources, impacts on stabilization and growth, and maintenance of freedom. These are goals in the sense that a nation's controlling forces in effect agree to have government produce these effects. Finally, in Chapters 8 through 10 we will consider the possibilities and limitations of some major tools for influencing public spending choices. One set of tools that has been much publicized in recent years includes cost-benefit analysis and program budgeting—tools intended to facilitate an economic calculus by decision makers. Another tool by means of which to alter decisions is the institutional framework, which can be manipulated. Indeed, as will be seen, an economic calculus to help identify the choices that one prefers will be of little use if the institutional arrangements lead to different choices. For this reason, the latter chapters will emphasize *both* steps to better spending decisions—the use of an economic calculus *and* the modification of institutions in government. The multilevel government structure is a special, and especially important, aspect of the institutional framework, and it is given separate attention.

I have for the most part neglected the interrelationship between taxing and spending policies,[9] though it is rarely clear just what the costs and gains from "factoring out" different pieces of a problem are. In any event, the study will pertain mainly to spending decisions as such.

---

[9] These interrelationships have been particularly stressed, and quite properly, by James M. Buchanan, "The Pure Theory of Government Finance: A Suggested Approach," *Journal of Political Economy*, December, 1949, pp. 496–505, and in his other writings.

two

PUBLIC SPENDING AND THE UNSEEN HAND IN GOVERNMENT

As Chapter 1 indicated, government spending is a critical element in people's lives. It is important for us to understand better how governmental spending decisions are reached, how the myriad choices are made. Who decided that the annual U.S. Federal budget would be approximately $100 billion in the early 1960s instead of $50 billion or $300 billion? How was it decided that U.S. governments would condone slavery until 1865 and provide Negroes with inferior governmental services most of the time thereafter? How does it happen that Federal benefits run a gamut from "Accidents, airplane" to "Zoological Park, National"?[1] Is there a social mind or collective will that knows how to reach the correct choices? If people would just elect the right officials, would the right decisions be made? To help answer such questions, one needs a theory of government to supplement the theory of the firm.[2]

No *precise* answers or theory can be given here

Note: Some of the materials in this chapter were included in "The Unseen Hand in Government," *American Economic Review*, June, 1965, pp. 496–505.

[1] *Encyclopedia of U.S. Government Benefits*, Wm. H. Wise & Co., Inc., New York.

[2] Important contributions from economics to a theory of government include James M. Buchanan and Gordon

(or elsewhere), but a general framework to show how group choices are made can be presented. This framework does not carry one very far, yet it can give some help in understanding what determines these decisions. It can direct one's attention to attainable imperfect worlds rather than (or in addition to) hypothetical utopias. A better understanding of the forces that shape government decisions is a part of positive science, for it can help us predict the consequences of alternative arrangements or actions. Coupled with personal judgments about untested hypotheses and about values, a better understanding of this process can also help each person decide what policies and institutional arrangements *he* prefers.

how governments reach decisions: utility maximization by individuals

Many persons have in their minds quite misleading images of government in action. To some, government suggests only smoke-filled rooms, corruption, inefficiency, and impending oppression. To others, government apparently means an impersonal device that will automatically act in the public interest. Moreover, since there is no agreed-upon conception of the public interest, each of these persons means *his* idea of the public interest. Thus many persons, especially when they say "The government should control this or that," apparently visualize government as an impersonal force that will automatically implement *their* policy ideas.

If one reflects on the matter a bit, however, it becomes apparent that neither of these extremes approaches reality. Government, whether municipal, state, or federal, is not an automatic machine for doing evil or good (or one man's conception of good). It is an activity carried on by people who are much like

Tullock, *The Calculus of Consent*, University of Michigan Press, Ann Arbor, Mich., 1962; Anthony Downs, *An Economic Theory of Democracy*, Harper & Row, Publishers, Incorporated, New York, 1957; C. E. Lindblom, *Bargaining: The Hidden Hand in Government*, The RAND Corporation, RM-1434, Santa Monica, Calif., 1955; C. E. Lindblom, *The Intelligence of Democracy*, The Free Press of Glencoe, New York, 1965; James G. March and Herbert A. Simon, *Organizations*, John Wiley & Sons, New York, 1958; Mancur Olson, Jr., *The Logic of Collective Action*, Harvard University Press, Cambridge, Mass., 1965; Herbert A. Simon, *Administrative Behavior*, 2d ed., The Macmillan Company, New York, 1961; Herbert A. Simon, Donald W. Smithburg, and Victor A. Thompson, *Public Administration*, Alfred A. Knopf, Inc., New York, 1950; Gordon Tullock, *The Politics of Bureaucracy*, Public Affairs Press, Washington, D.C., 1965; Alan Williams, "The Optimal Provision of Public Goods in a System of Local Government," *Journal of Political Economy*, February, 1966, pp. 18–33. For a review of other pertinent literature, see Richard A. Musgrave, *The Theory of Public Finance*, McGraw-Hill Book Company, New York, 1959, pp. 116–135. Needless to say, there are many significant contributions in political science, some of which are cited in Buchanan and Tullock, *op. cit.*

the rest of us. Furthermore, spending choices result from *individual* decisions—those of voters, legislators, the heads of departments or ministries, departmental employees, and so on. Each individual involved in this process has somewhat different views and values from the others—that is, he has to take his own, or what might be called a parochial, viewpoint. At the same time he must reckon with the viewpoints of the others. In taking his stand and deciding what action (if any) he will take, he considers the wishes of others, expressed or sensed, and the rewards offered and penalties threatened by others. The Secretary of Agriculture cannot act without any regard for the views of his subordinates, the White House, and Congress; and congressmen and the President cannot form their positions completely without regard for the attitudes of voters, other congressmen, and departmental officials. Consequently, spending decisions are the result of a network of conflicting views and considerations.[3] Individuals, not mysterious group entities, make decisions, yet those choices are by no means independent of other persons' views. Similarly, in a bowl of marbles, individual marbles, rather than groups, move; but the movement of each marble depends upon the positions and movements of the others.

The forming of a budget, for example, is a complex sort of bargaining game (and indeed "gaming" such activities might alter naïve beliefs about government). All branch chiefs and officials should believe in the importance of their responsibilities, or they ought not be in their positions. For this and other reasons, most officials believe that the activities under their supervision ought to be expanded. In proposing a budget, however, they must consider the reactions of their subordinates, equals, and superiors, the Budget Bureau, and the Congress. On the one hand, an official can usually be sure that his budget will be cut, and he may "pad" it to allow for such cuts. On the other hand, if he asks for "too much," he may precipitate conflicts with fellow officials, damage his reputation for good judgment, and end up with a budget smaller than that which would have resulted from a more modest request. Higher officials, in turn, have great difficulty in appraising these requests. They feel great pressure from one source or another to expand some outlays; they feel less pressure concerning others[4]—and improved information about the effects of any outlay is costly for each official to obtain. Even after the appropriations have been approved, the specific spending choices that remain open are shaped by similar

---

[3] See, for example, Arthur Smithies, *The Budgetary Process in the United States*, McGraw-Hill Book Company, New York, 1955; Edward C. Banfield, *Political Influence*, Free Press of Glencoe, New York, 1961; Aaron Wildavsky, *The Politics of the Budgetary Process*, Little, Brown and Company, Boston, 1964.

[4] Wildavsky has an excellent discussion of the way various positions are formed and decisions are reached (*op. cit.*, pp. 63–126).

bargaining and weighing processes. How much to have left at the end of the fiscal year is not an easy decision for officials to make, for they are subject to criticism if they have too much left, if they turn to Congress for a supplement, or if they come out exactly even. At all levels, choices are made by individuals —persons who are inevitably constrained by their limited capacities and parochial viewpoints, yet concerned (for a variety of reasons) about the wishes of others.

It is helpful to visualize each individual as a utility maximizer who reaches his decisions on the basis of a cost-benefit balance sheet, or "T-account." Each person—whether acting as a member of a household, as a businessman, or as a governmental official—seeks what might be called "preferredness" or "utility" in life. Each individual adjusts or makes decisions so as to maximize his utility as he sees it. In other words his behavior is generally purposeful, not random.[5] He takes those actions that he believes to be best. This does not imply that he is highly hedonistic, selfish, callous, materialistic, immoral, or anything of the sort. The thousands of items that contribute to an individual's "utility" in this sense include helping others, performing tasks well, playing and relaxing, exploring ideas, enjoying beautiful scenery and works of art, enjoying peace of mind, and adhering to moral codes and ethical rules—as well as having personal comfort, material goods, prestige, and so on. Selfishness means attaching a higher value to helping oneself than helping others.[6] Utility maximization simply means choosing purposefully in view of whatever utility a person ascribes to the things he wants (or doesn't want) and deems attainable.

How does an individual choose among alternative actions, then? He weighs the costs or sacrifices of utility entailed by each action against the gains in utility provided by that action. Suppose he is considering the purchase of a pair of shoes. First he must decide how much time and effort he will devote to acquiring information about different brands and types of shoes. For instance, he must decide whether or not to prepare an explicit cost-gain analysis of various brands. Intuitively—and in a fraction of a second—he elects not to

---

[5] One of the best short presentations of the utility-maximization hypothesis is by Armen A. Alchian, "Private Property and the Relative Cost of Tenure," in Philip D. Bradley (ed.), *The Public Stake in Union Power*, University of Virginia Press, Charlottesville, Va., 1958, pp. 350–371. See also Armen A. Alchian and William R. Allen, *University Economics*, 2d ed., Wadsworth Publishing Co., Inc., Belmont, Calif., 1967, chap. 2; and Gary S. Becker, *The Economics of Discrimination*, The University of Chicago Press, Chicago, 1957.

[6] It is interesting to speculate on what the world would be like if human beings had quite different utility functions from those they apparently have at present. Personally, I doubt if any large group could long survive if most of its members were either *extremely* selfish or *extremely* unselfish.

do so. Implicitly he has consulted a T-account pertaining to one of the alternative actions:

Making a formal analysis of various shoes

COSTS	GAINS
Utility of the time and convenience sacrificed	Utility of trivial probability of making slightly better choice

In this example he judges, without thinking about it in formal terms, that the costs of the action would exceed the gains.

Most individual choices are made in this fashion, that is, without any formal or even conscious analysis (often guided by rules of thumb that are believed to be economical). In other words, intuitive cost-gain analysis often tells one that detailed analysis would not be worthwhile. Nonetheless, the individual *is* choosing those courses of action that he thinks will yield more gain than cost.[7] And often an individual does turn to *conscious* comparison of alternatives and sometimes to *explicit* analyses on paper. In all instances, though, the relevant considerations can be conceived of in the form of a balance sheet or T-account. For instance, a person may list the pros and cons of a new job opportunity:

Accepting position as manager of gambling house in Community X

COSTS	GAINS
Disutility of sacrificing present salary, working conditions, climate, friendships and associations, community, recreational facilities, etc.	Utility of new salary and (highly uncertain) working conditions, climate, friendships and associations, etc.
Disutility of departing from individual's moral code	Utility of ready access to quiet, beautiful wilderness area
Disutility of losing esteem in certain quarters because of new occupation	

Note that this example involves the utility attached to the feelings of others (esteem, in this instance), the utility of maintaining or violating a moral code, and the utility of numerous other nonmaterial factors. Such considerations are extremely important in many choices. Violating an ethical rule, for example, is

---

[7] The psychologist would use different terminology, perhaps that people seek "gratifications" and try to avoid "deprivations."

so costly to many individuals that they never, at least in ordinary circumstances, consider many possible actions such as cheating or stealing.

Note too that, even in the simplest illustrations, the *probabilities* of various consequences figure importantly in assessing their utilities or disutilities. No matter how much anyone values personal promotion or civil rights, he may not be moved to take an action to further those aims if the action has a near-zero probability of having any effect. Everyone has an enormous stake in preventing thermonuclear war, but few persons put in several hours a day in efforts to prevent it. Why? Because they know that individual efforts of ordinary persons can have almost no influence on the probability of such a war. This is one reason why many motives that might be called noble ones play rather small roles in shaping the vast majority of decisions.

Businessmen too behave as utility maximizers, and they too may be concerned about aesthetics, moral rules, kindness to others, community opinion, the reactions of regulatory commissions, their personal tastes, the tastes of their wives, and the beauty of female employees—as well as about the present values of their firms.[8] If competition is vigorous and if major stockholders can obtain information at moderate cost, managers will have to concentrate *mainly* on increasing profits (or reducing losses) so as to increase the present worths of their firms, but accurate T-accounts pertaining to business decisions will nonetheless involve *numerous* variables affecting the decision makers' own personal utilities.

Every participant in governmental processes can also be regarded as a utility maximizer. Each voter goes through some sort of cost-gain calculus in making up his mind about whether he approves of a proposed program or action. It is usually economical for these appraisals to be rough, hasty, intuitive calculations, though the potential stakes or cost-reward structures sometimes impel people to scribble on the back of an envelope or even to prepare systematic analyses. One might say that millions of individuals daily consult thousands of little cost-gain T-accounts as they seek preferred situations. Each person's decisions are based, not on one particular aspect of an action (e.g., its contribution to the nation's GNP, or the utility to this person of its contribution to GNP, or the utility of the action's impact on the probability of maintaining "freedom"), but on weighing *all* the gains in utility against *all* the costs—*as that person perceives them.*

Frequently, of course, a preliminary and intuitive calculus tells a citizen that

---

[8] Armen A. Alchian and Reuben A. Kessel, "Competition, Monopoly, and the Pursuit of Money," in *Aspects of Labor Economics*, A Universities National Bureau Conference, Princeton University Press, Princeton, N.J., 1962, pp. 157–175.

the prospects of getting helpful information, of understanding the issue, and especially of influencing the outcome make it uneconomical to devote even a minute to thinking about a proposed outlay. After all, not many persons assiduously scan each year's Federal budget to decide whether or not they approve of each line item. A citizen may decide to ignore the matter; to adopt a simple rule of thumb, such as "Whatever position Joe takes is the one I'll take"; to write letters and be active in organizations supporting his views; or to vote a straight party ticket. (Imperfect rules like following slogans, voting according to labels or other crude indicators, and thinking in stereotypes often make sense as soon as one recognizes that information is costly. As misleading as broad labels are, they still may be better than the attainable alternatives.)

Thus, on a particular issue, many voters decide to do nothing and pass on to the next cost-gain calculus (perhaps whether to watch Danny Kaye or the late movie). Some decide to watch the newspapers or chat with a friend to get more information. Some form an opinion but decide that no action that occurs to them would be worthwhile. Some put the information in their memory drums for future reference in dealing with future choices. Some will refer to it, for example, when making their intuitive cost-gain calculus about whether to vote for Congressman X. A few feel strongly enough about the issue to take other kinds of action.

Each union leader, head of an organization such as the U.S. Chamber of Commerce or the League of Women Voters, publisher, and television commentator goes through his cost-gain calculus in deciding what he will say or do. He will usually find that one particular element—the impact of his decisions on the approval or support of others—is more important in his calculus than it is for the man in the street. His utility depends to a considerable extent on the reactions of his followers and potential followers, readers, audience, customers, colleagues, employer, and potential employers. This is not to his discredit. He has to take into account the views of persons other than himself (and few of us would, in the long run, want an arrangement in which he could act completely independently).

When we turn to politicians, legislators, and government officials, we find still more emphasis placed on gaining approval or support. These persons are the sellers—legislators being more like manufacturers, agency officials being more like retailers—of packages of utilities such as defense or antipoverty programs. Their cost-gain statements or T-accounts[9] are filled with items like gains

---

[9] For illustrative T-accounts regarding a proposed action from the standpoints of a mayor and an alderman, see Roland N. McKean, "Costs and Benefits from Different Viewpoints," in Howard G. Schaller (ed.), *Public Expenditure Decisions in the Urban Community,* Resources for the Future, Washington, D.C., 1963, pp. 147–162. For some of the elements in the utility functions of school officials, see Neal Gross, *Who Runs Our Schools?* John Wiley & Sons, Inc., New York, 1958.

or losses of votes, gains or losses of support for their respective proposals, and gains or losses of time and convenience in dealing with colleagues and pressure groups. In addition, of course, their utility functions include items like gains or losses in nongovernment business activities resulting from the reactions of various persons; gains and losses because of their sentiments, principles, sincere wishes to help the underprivileged, or their conceptions of the national interest; and gains and losses in terms of empire building and its effects on prestige, authority, income, and future prospects. And this only scratches the surface as far as the list of variables is concerned.

In a real sense the job of politicians, legislators, and government officials, like that of businessmen, is to arrange advantageous trades. If they make poor deals, they lose part of their power to influence future decisions and make advantageous trades. If they lose too much of this power, they do not survive in government. For this reason legislators and high officials, somewhat like executives in the private sector, must be especially concerned about one variable—pleasing the "customer," i.e., the voter—in order to survive and keep life tolerably free from criticism. And, like employees in the private sector, government employees must usually have some concern about pleasing their superiors in order to hold their jobs or seek promotion or at least maintain tolerable working conditions. In government the linkage is usually looser, and officials probably have more discretion, at least in certain directions, than business executives. Nonetheless, in Western democracies, a good deal depends ultimately upon the results of utility maximization by voters.

So far, the discussion amounts to no more than a tautology. To say that individuals maximize utility is to say that a man acts because of the things that make him act. Such statements can explain any behavior but predict no particular behavior. The actions of both a Buddhist monk and a gangster are consistent with utility maximization. With some supplementary propositions, however, the analysis of utility maximization can be a powerful tool to use in examining governmental decisions. The thousands of elements in utility functions—the items that yield utility—are in varying degrees substitutes for each other. Some amount of Effect A will compensate a person for giving up a unit of Effect B. Some of these elements can be identified, as was done above, and then one can apply the basic proposition in economics—the law of demand—which says that the more expensive anything is, the fewer units will be demanded, and the less expensive an item is, the larger the quantity demanded. If the cost to an individual of one item increases, other things are less expensive relative to that item; he will demand less of it and more of other things. If the gain from one item increases, other things are relatively more expensive than they were before; more of this item will be demanded and less of others. If an input becomes more costly, it will be used more sparingly. If one's time becomes more valuable than it formerly was *(ceteris paribus)*, he will make fewer or less careful explicit cost-gain analyses pertaining to minor decisions. In government, if the cost to an official of an action increases, he will take less of it, and if the gains increase (in votes or colleague support or anything that has utility for him), he will take more action of that sort.

The passage of any piece of legislation or the reaching of almost any decision can illustrate the point. If it becomes easier to obtain funds, an official will demand more. If a strong coalition of senators forms in opposition to a bill, that is, if the cost of passing it increases, the original advocates will compromise, i.e., demand a smaller quantity. The law of demand applies even to factors such as moral principles. Most people believe that it is immoral to kill people, and some attach an infinite value to adhering to this rule. But many people will kill if the cost of not doing so is being killed or allowing five more persons to be killed. And some who would not kill one man to prevent five others from being killed would do so to save a hundred lives. That is, some individuals at the margin take less of "not killing" if its cost increases.

Perhaps it should be emphasized again that selfishness on the part of voters or government officials is *not* implied. What is implied is that the less expensive a charitable action is, the more of it will be taken. If charitable donations are made deductible for tax purposes, one would expect more donations. If the hospital is 5 miles away, good Samaritans will drive sick strangers to the hospital more frequently than they will if the hospital is 50 miles away. If voting on the basis of sentiment costs a congressman a hundred votes, it will happen more frequently than it will if it costs a thousand votes.

This point is not new (though it is too often neglected); Adam Smith long ago discussed the implications of the law of demand in nonmarket institutional settings.[10] He thought about the effects of different property arrangements, ways of remunerating judges and government personnel, and the effects of the cost-reward structures in churches and universities. According to Smith, if clerks were paid according to the number of written pages produced, they would write many pages; and if army chiefs or politicians were not restrained by countervailing power, they would behave in antisocial ways. And he attributed bad outcomes not to bad people but to institutional frameworks that failed to recognize the power of self-interest (i.e., utility maximization).

Needless to say, a change in the probability of success can alter the costs or gains felt by decision makers. If the chances of getting Congressman A's proposal enacted fall almost to zero, A will not gain much from B's help and will not offer much for it. As the possible rewards to B decline, B will exert less

---

[10] Nathan Rosenberg, "Some Institutional Aspects of the *Wealth of Nations*," *Journal of Political Economy*, December, 1960, pp. 557–570.

PUBLIC SPENDING AND THE UNSEEN HAND IN GOVERNMENT

effort to support A's proposal. In 1956, when support for two Republican leaders in Philadelphia became almost evenly divided, the worth of having the aid of a few more ward leaders rose, and "large bribes were reportedly offered to wavering ward leaders, and it is said that several of them were threatened with physical violence."[11] This example happens to involve actions that most persons would regard as undesirable, but the point applies to any choice: a shift in the probability that a cost or gain will occur affects the utility of the action contemplated.

The outlook for any kind of government that is responsive to large numbers of the people may seem bleak when one allows for the high cost to individuals of seeking information, of thinking carefully, and of taking various actions, and when one allows for the low utility to an individual of a slim chance of affecting anything. There may be a similarity here to the functioning of the price mechanism, however: for the latter mechanism to work, it isn't necessary for *all* buyers to alter their behavior when a price changes—the important thing is for *some* consumers to be on the margin and to respond. Similarly, for the voting-bargaining mechanism to be effective, it may not be essential for a high percentage of citizens to ponder *all* issues and take action. If the costs of response are low enough that *some* persons are near the margin on most issues, it may still make for a fairly responsive system.

the bargaining mechanism as an unseen hand

Utility maximization by individuals coupled with bargaining and exchange may tend toward a sensible pattern of decisions and resource use.[12] Specific outcomes depend upon the structure of rights and the rules governing exchange, but in general the bargaining mechanism in the public sector has effects that are somewhat similar to those of the price and exchange mechanism in the private sector. Both mechanisms tend to substitute voluntary exchange for direct coercion and induce decision makers to take into account many of the indirect or external impacts of their decisions. Of course, government possesses great coercive power, and its actions inevitably coerce individuals or minorities (sometimes the majority) to a considerable extent. But bargaining can reduce the extent to which this is so.

---

[11] James Reichley, *The Art of Government: Reform and Organizational Policies in Philadelphia*, A Report to the Fund for the Republic, reprinted from *Greater Philadelphia Magazine*, Philadelphia, Pa. (no date), footnote 21, p. 14.

[12] Interesting contributions to our understanding of this process have been made in connection with sociology and biology. See George C. Homans, *Sentiments and Activities*, The Free Press of Glencoe, New York, 1962; and Nicolas Rashevsky, *Mathematical Biology of Social Behavior*, rev. ed., The University of Chicago Press, Chicago, 1959.

In the private sector, the price mechanism makes individuals feel many of the relevant costs and gains implied by their decisions. When a business firm takes action, it has to bargain with and compensate numerous persons who supply rights to use buildings, labor services, and other inputs. That is, if the firm's action uses up or damages property, the firm ordinarily has to buy the consent of the owners. Whenever the firm's action produces beneficial effects, the management tries to charge the beneficiaries. If all compensations are made and the firm still makes a profit, some persons are made better off without making others worse off. The greater the extent to which all these compensations are made, the less the extent to which the firm's costs and gains will diverge from total costs and gains.

In government the bargaining mechanism produces some of the same effects. If a public official's action will use up someone's property or damage certain interests, he will probably find a cost associated with that action. He will feel the complaints of those damaged or the inconvenience of trying to mollify them. Or the cost may be embarrassing or expensive enmities among his colleagues or retaliation by other officials. He has to bargain with many people that are affected and, in one way or another, encounter costs if he makes decisions that impose sacrifices on others. From those who are benefited, on the other hand, he can bargain for compensation. The reward may be support in connection with other matters, reduced enmity, increased friendship or convenience, or some other kind of *quid pro quo*. The size and completeness of the compensations for both costs inflicted and gains bestowed depend upon bargaining strengths, transaction costs, and circumstances (as they do in the private economy). And again the greater the extent to which these compensations are made, the less the extent to which the costs and gains felt by an official will diverge from total costs and gains.

Every decision or action, it might be noted, involves bargaining, tacit or explicit. If a husband goes bowling by himself and it adversely affects his family's plans, he pays either by incurring their displeasure or by feeling that he owes them a favor. If the latter, the family collects when the occasion arises. If one asks a colleague to criticize a paper or asks a neighbor to water his lawn, there is a little IOU involved. As Homans says, our understanding "would be furthered by our adopting the view that interaction between persons is an exchange of goods, material and nonmaterial. This is one of the oldest theories of social behavior, and one that we still use every day to interpret our own behavior, as when we say, 'I found so-and-so rewarding.'... But, perhaps just because it is so obvious, this view has been much neglected by social scientists...."[13]

---

[13] Homans, *op. cit.*, p. 279.

If a government official speaks or votes against a Federal grant-in-aid program or an increase in the minimum wage, he receives the favor of some persons and colleagues and the antagonism of others. He makes this bargain when he decides to act (or not to act, as the case may be). When a senator considers voting to censure Senator X, he asks himself, "What will be the consequences?" If he decides to accept the reactions of others to his "yes" vote, *that* is his bargain. If he decides to refrain from voting or to vote no, he accepts a different set of reactions, and *that* is his trade. Much of the bargaining is tacit. A departmental official who allocates the budget among projects or awards contracts or recommends higher interest rates on Rural Electrification Administration loans does not necessarily receive many phone calls from congressmen or the White House. If he has average intelligence, he has a good idea of which senators will be angry at alternative decisions, which ones will be pleased, and so on, just as a consumer knows approximately what a pair of shoes will cost—without any telephone calls. Sometimes, of course, one makes mistakes; and part of the time explicit haggling occurs.

As in the private sector, shifts in costs or gains (that is, prices paid or received) cause shifts in behavior. As conditions change, the price of apples sometimes goes up and the price of oranges down. Consumers alter their behavior, though not necessarily their nature. Similarly, if a senator from Texas becomes President of the United States, the price or cost of some actions goes up and the cost of other actions goes down. And the structure of rewards alters. For example, the cost of closing down a base in New York goes up; the cost of closing an installation in Texas goes down. The rewards for a war on poverty across the entire United States go up; those for aid to constituents in a particular state go down. Thus, the man who becomes President will take a more nearly national viewpoint—that is, will acquire a broader sense of responsibility—though his nature need not change at all. The altered cost-reward structures are bound to affect his behavior. Like the price system, this bargaining mechanism has many effects that most persons would regard as desirable. It might be called the "unseen hand in government."[14]

Examples of the bargaining mechanism at work are abundant. President Lyndon Johnson's Great Society programs appeared to stem from a shift in the price to officials of approving such measures. Johnson's tremendous victory in 1964 was like a sweeping change of price tags; the rewards to congressmen (in terms of votes and support) for favoring these programs went up, and the cost of favoring them went down. Bargaining brought many interesting extras. For example, in a close struggle over the rent-subsidy program, Senator E. L. Bart-

---

[14] C. E. Lindblom, *Bargaining: The Hidden Hand in Government*, The RAND Corporation, RM-1434, 1955.

lett of Alaska at first withheld his support. He "suddenly received promises that the administration would arrange loans for Eskimos, Aleuts and Indians living in Alaska's remote Arctic regions—a pet project on which he had hitherto received not a scintilla of White House encouragement. After voting for rent subsidies [which were approved 46 to 45], Bartlett confessed: 'I'm not proud of myself. It's not the kind of thing I normally do.'"[15] But this behavior is not necessarily reprehensible. How else can minorities or groups with strong special tastes make their preferences felt? In all likelihood it would be far worse for most of us if an administration had so much power that it did not have to bargain with anyone! Trades of this sort are to be expected, they are essential to the process of making government responsive to diverse groups of citizens, and their effects are not *all* bad.

Thus, while the particular values, principles, or even whims of a government official occasionally play roles in his decisions, they do not usually play major roles in democratic governments.[16] The bargaining mechanism limits the discretion of decision makers. Let us look at this side of the coin—the constraints on the authority of individual officials. Again the forces at work are akin to those that operate in the private sector. In a highly competitive industry, a business firm must give much attention to avoiding losses and increasing profits, or it will fail.[17] In these circumstances, employees find that they must devote most of their efforts to achieving the firm's goals or be fired. In a public utility or nonprofit corporation, both managers and employees have greater leeway, but they too are limited in the extent to which altruistic, evil, or personal aims can guide their actions. In government also, while managers and other personnel have some discretion, they cannot completely flout the wishes of voters, superiors, and colleagues, and hope to survive for long. They certainly cannot do just whatever they wish. They must compromise with their principles, whether good or evil, and accept a great deal of guidance from the unseen hand.

The fact that individual decision makers have parochial viewpoints—the fact that they do not ask each morning, "What can I do for GNP today?"—does not mean that the pattern of decisions will inevitably be stupid or vicious. The right kind of bargaining process can make special interests and parochial viewpoints, which one might think would produce chaotic decisions, lead to an orderly and sensible pattern of choices. If well designed, the unseen hand can

---

[15] *Time,* May 6, 1966.

[16] Bargaining also exists, of course, in an authoritarian government. With each different arrangement regarding rights and rules for bargaining, however, decisions are responsive to different groups, and the outcomes are different.

[17] Firms have leeway for considerable periods of time, but the lower the profits and the higher the losses, the greater the probability of failure.

go a long way toward turning private vice into public virtue in government as well as in the private sector.

Some persons believe that individuals are rather selfish. In interpreting past events, one historian noted, "Men went into Parliament 'to make a figure,' and no more dreamt of a seat in the House to benefit humanity than a child dreams of a birthday cake that others may eat it; which is perfectly normal and in no way reprehensible."[18] Here, however, it is not essential to pass judgment on the degree of selfishness. What is essential is to recognize that there are both selfish and altruistic elements in people's utility functions, but that institutional arrangements can often make undesirable behavior relatively expensive (and over the centuries this occurred, to some extent, with respect to members of Parliament and officialdom in many nations).

The bargaining mechanism may seem exceedingly crude since government decision making appears to cater to majorities rather than to individual preferences, and it appears to respond to voters' views on packages of issues rather than on individual issues (let alone *increments* in particular proposals). Perhaps the best one can hope for is government of the people, by some of the people, and for the majority of the people. But the mechanism is not quite as imprecise as that. Minority views on particular issues carry some weight with government officials because there is the threat that minority-group voters, when considering the larger package of issues at election time, may shift their votes and in effect form a new coalition having real power. Differential intensity of feelings or different values attached to particular policies can carry weight for essentially the same reason. As noted above in connection with Senator Bartlett's action, if a minority attaches a high value to a particular policy, it can sacrifice its feelings about other issues and join the coalition of its choice. Others react, as they see the prices being paid for various decisions, by accepting a little less of those items that are becoming relatively expensive and a little more of those items that are becoming relatively cheap. In legislative bodies, similarly, views on individual issues as opposed to a package, the views of minorities, and differences in the values attached to particular policies do help shape decisions, because some trade-offs—giving up a vote on this issue for someone else's vote on that one, giving up some of one policy for more of another—are possible, and "shadow prices," so to speak, gradually emerge to reveal the costs and gains from various actions. Because there are checks and balances, a multiplicity of interests represented in the bargaining process, and some possibilities for volun-

---

[18] Sir Lewis Namier, *Crossroads of Power*, St. Martin's Press, Inc., New York, 1962. Namier's point was also made in an entertaining fashion by the British movie, *I'm All Right, Jack*, which showed laborers, shop stewards, executives, and government officials all trying to advance their personal interests in the light of the constraints.

tary exchange, the pattern of choices can cater to individual preferences better than may be suggested by the words "majority rule."

This bargaining mechanism has *some* influence on most choices, though the extent of this influence varies greatly with circumstances.[19] In the aggregate these choices and decisions shape the allocation of resources at various levels. Consider first the allocation of resources between the private and public sectors. Suppose a larger share for government is under consideration. Senators and congressmen will become aware of constituents' views on this and other issues and will respond to prospective votes almost the way a board of directors responds to prospective profits. These legislators will "feel" many of the expected benefits and costs.

Second, consider the allocation of resources within the public sector among programs and activities (comparable to the allocation of resources among industries). Officials can take home no profits, and they are spending other people's money; yet they may "feel" the major gains and costs because some trade-offs are possible and crude "shadow prices" emerge from the bargaining process. An official finds that it not only rewards him but also costs him something to expand his program. Resources tend to be shifted toward programs in which marginal individual benefit (MIB) is greater than marginal individual cost (MIC); bargaining helps make MIB equal to MTB (marginal total benefit) and MIC equal to MTC (marginal total cost).[20] The unseen hand harnesses individual decisions so that they come a little closer than they otherwise would to satisfying the "welfare equation":

$$MTC = MIC = MIB = MTB[21]$$

Finally, consider the utilization of resources within a program by lower-level officials (comparable to the allocation of resources by firms within an industry). The alternative methods of production that are considered depend upon constraints that proscribe certain of the alternatives and pressures that induce per-

---

[19] For example, such influence is much smaller wherever decision makers are partially sheltered from the necessity of bargaining, e.g., the Supreme Court or agencies that are relatively independent. Such independent checks and balances, however, can often play a beneficial role in the overall bargaining network.

[20] Although it may be a small semantic issue, I prefer to talk of "total" costs and benefits, which suggest that they are felt by individuals, instead of "social" costs and benefits, which may sound as though some mysterious entity like the state feels these effects.

[21] A classic presentation pertaining to the welfare equations and to discrepancies in the private sector is that of A. P. Lerner in *The Economics of Control*, The Macmillan Company, New York, 1944, chap. 6, pp. 72–77.

As will be stressed in the next chapter, while fulfilling these conditions has a certain kind of appeal, one need not regard their fulfillment as desirable; there is no ultimate test for correct actions from the "group's" standpoint.

sonnel to examine more or fewer alternatives. The costs and gains from each alternative, as perceived by government personnel, depend upon the criteria in terms of which those personnel are judged by their superiors, which depend in turn on the pressures that those superiors feel. Again the gears of the mechanism may appear to clank quite a bit; but rivalry and the bargaining process still cause personnel to feel some effects that they might otherwise neglect. The process still works to make gross inefficiency somewhat costly to government personnel. To some extent, flagrant inefficiency impairs an official's ability to bargain for promotion, larger budgets, freedom from investigation, and other desiderata. Compared with discretionary authority, then, the bargaining mechanism is again a valuable and unseen hand guiding resource utilization.

divergences between individual and total costs and gains

In both the private and the public sectors, however, these bargaining mechanisms are imperfect. All costs and gains are not felt by decision makers and therefore do not get taken into account properly. In other words, in both sectors there are divergences between the costs and gains from the standpoint of individual decision makers and those from the standpoint of others. Such divergences are often called "externalities" or "spillovers." In the private sphere, for example, an airline may not include among its costs the damages to other businesses or to households caused by noise (unless protests, threat of lawsuit, or governmental regulation cause the firm to take such costs into account). An individual automobile operator is unlikely to include among his costs the contribution he makes to congestion or smog. Similarly, the bargaining mechanism in government is far from perfect, and a governmental unit or individual official may neglect costs inflicted or gains bestowed on others. Third parties who have little or no bargaining power are often affected. Public officials may not be induced to bring MTC very close to MTB. In recent years, for example, Socialist countries have become greatly disturbed because the bargaining mechanism does not induce managers of manufacturing enterprises to maximize what it is believed they should maximize.[22] The same thing is presumably true, however, of other Socialist (and non-Socialist) public officials. They too are managers of enterprises; the main difference is that the quality and quantity of their outputs are harder to observe or measure.

In both the private and the public sectors, the extent of the divergences de-

---

[22] See, for instance, Janos Kornai, *Overcentralization in Economic Administration: A Critical Analysis Based on Experience in Hungarian Light Industry*, trans. John Knapp, Oxford University Press, Fair Lawn, N.J., 1959; or Myron E. Sharpe (ed.), *The Liberman Discussion: A New Phase in Soviet Economic Thought*, International Arts and Sciences Press, White Plains, N.Y., 1966.

pends upon the institutional arrangements. In the private sphere it depends partly upon how well property rights are defined and enforced or upon how well government regulations work. Thus, noise and exhaust gases cause divergences because it is difficult to define property rights to noise-free and smog-free air, and it is extremely expensive to exclude nonpayers or to negotiate and enforce contracts regarding such rights.[23] Hence it is not economical for people to charge airlines and automobile drivers for using this valuable resource (or for the vehicle owners to charge householders for *not* using the air), and the impact is not voluntarily accepted in an exchange on any market. If *no* property rights were enforced, if theft and coercion were freely permitted, spillovers would be very great indeed. (Although individual property rights are believed by some to generate selfishness, they can be viewed, and may have originated, as a device to *prevent* people from selfishly ignoring the costs they impose on others.) In the public sector, too, institutional arrangements and transaction costs[24] have much to do with the extent of these divergences between individual costs or gains and total costs or gains. If local governments do not have to bargain with each other, one community may dispose of its sewage so as to impose costs on others. If a metropolitan government consisted of councilmen elected at large, the majority might well ignore the wants of minorities or local areas and the costs thrust upon them. A metropolitan government with councilmen elected from various districts would probably be less likely to neglect such spillovers.

A more formal way of describing the situation is as follows: To many decision makers and organizations the marginal individual cost of an action *(MIC)* diverges from the marginal total cost *(MTC)*, and the marginal individual benefit *(MIB)* differs from the marginal total benefit *(MTB)*. There are plenty of examples of divergences between *MIC* and *MTC*, and between *MIB* and *MTB*, in the public sector. Relatively poor communities are often glad to have the state or federal governments pay part of the costs of certain local programs and may approve such programs only if the costs can be partially shifted to others. Relatively wealthy communities, on the other hand, may oppose state or federal help, because the "spill-in" cost of other cities' programs (via higher state and Federal taxes) might make *their* costs exceed the gains they feel.[25] On the

[23] These matters will be considered more fully in Chapter 5.
[24] See later references to the work of Harold Demsetz.
[25] For an interesting case study and discussion of these matters, see Werner Z. Hirsch, Elbert Segelhorst, and Morton J. Marcus, *Spillover of Public Education Costs and Benefits*, Institute of Government and Public Affairs, University of California, Los Angeles, Calif., 1964.

benefit side, a community may ignore gains bestowed on other communities in deciding whether or not to provide recreational facilities or high-quality schools. The spillover benefits may occur because of persistent migration, because of trade or cultural contacts, or because of impacts on delinquency, crime, and general security. The community will take some of these spillovers into account if it is compensated by some higher governmental unit or if communities bargain with each other. (In 1964 one city in Los Angeles County decided not to have its annual fireworks display, but an adjoining city said that it reaped benefits too; so, after some haggling, compensation was arranged and the fireworks display was presented.)

Similar problems of spillovers or interdependencies exist at higher levels of government. It is often said that Federal-agency officials who are responsible for supplies feel the costs of being caught short more than the costs of holding excessive inventories. On the other hand, if inventory management is placed in the hands of a central supply agency that has an incentive to minimize losses, the management may neglect the gains from hedging against crises and contingencies. In either case, the costs and rewards of inventory decisions as perceived by decision makers may diverge noticeably from total costs and gains. The actions of one department often affect the costs or gains from the actions of other parts of government. Thus, in constructing dams in Colorado, the Department of the Interior may affect the costs of the Agriculture Department's price-support programs, the costs of Arizona's and California's water-supply activities, the quality of downstream water, and the costs of individual firms and farmers. The Public Health Service hospital at Staten Island, New York, has allegedly been putting 7,500 gallons of untreated sewage per day into Upper New York Bay and also placing heavy burdens on New York City's regular sanitation system. Numerous military installations impose costs on local communities by discharging large quantities of sewage and industrial wastes into harbors and streams; for example, the Navy's Air Material Center in Philadelphia is said to have put huge quantities of wastes into the Delaware River. On the gain side, additional outlays for the Army's limited-war forces increase the worth of the airlift and sea lift programs of the Air Force and Navy, but this fact may not figure importantly in the Army's calculations.

At the congressional level—indeed in any part of government—there are difficulties with spillovers. The costs and gains from the Arkansas River project as viewed by its supporters must have diverged greatly from the total costs and gains as seen from the nation's standpoint. Furthermore, when Federal agencies consider the formulation of their budgets, they may be more concerned with getting the budgets increased than with counting costs and gains to the nation.

Political parties, which play important roles in the public sector, also tend to take parochial positions.[26]

In the international sphere (where officials and statesmen also behave as utility maximizers), the bargaining mechanism permits disastrous spillovers. Needless to say, foreign ministers and military leaders must look at costs and gains from their individual standpoints, and these are shaped largely by the pressures placed on them by people within their nations. Even if they wished to do so, they could not attempt to seek "world interest" or to maximize GWP (Kenneth Boulding's semifacetious term, "Gross World Product"). But the international scene is like an economy in which theft, compulsion, and violence are permissible, and divergences between individual and total costs or gains are staggering. Given the uncertainties that exist, the utility of making war often exceeds the utility of alternative policies *from the standpoint of individual nations*. It is a wildly expensive arrangement and accounts for many public spending choices. Unfortunately, alternative institutional arrangements might also turn out to be exceedingly costly (in other ways) to many peoples of the world.

These spillovers in the public sector, like those in the private sector, can be viewed as stemming from difficulties in defining and enforcing property rights. The rights of individual officials and nongovernment personnel to certain resources and their services are ill-defined. The governmental decision makers have no right to capture certain gains they produce, but they do have rights to avoid part of the costs they cause. Even if all rights could be neatly defined and assigned, the costs of excluding nonpayers from using resources and the costs of negotiating and enforcing innumerable contracts would be extremely high. Inside the public sector itself, then, regulations and constraints on various parts of government are introduced in an effort to cope with side effects. Here too people grope for those regulations, bargaining arrangements, and rules of thumb that appear to yield more gain than cost—though often they make mistakes.

One cannot be dogmatic, however, about the extent to which costs or gains are taken into account. A great deal of empirical work is in order, because not much is really known about the costs and gains to various utility maximizers where markets do not exist. Persons in government feel costs and gains attributable to their choices mostly through bargaining pressures, and these are hard to measure. Parochial outlooks as such do not reveal what costs or gains are felt. In the private sector, a businessman does not say, "I want to be sure and

---

[26] For differences between the parties on economic policies, and for ways in which bargaining pressures modify platforms and policies, see Seymour E. Harris, *The Economics of the Political Parties*, The Macmillan Company, New York, 1962.

take into account *all* the costs to the nation," and an uncritical observer might conclude that there must therefore be tremendous externalities. But the price system compels the businessman to consider most of the costs he causes. In the public sector, similarly, a government official does not say, "I want to be sure and count all the costs to the nation." Again a naïve observer might conclude that there must therefore be great externalities. But the bargaining process compels the official to take at least many of the costs into account. In short, too little is known about the process. For example, do voters and officials perceive gains from better schools differently in towns that are being deserted by the younger generation (so that the towns reap fewer of the benefits of the educational program) from the way the gains are perceived in communities that are growing? How *much* bargaining pressure does a city council feel to consider the costs that its behavior imposes on an adjacent community?

Nor can one therefore be dogmatic about the *net* ill effect of apparent divergences between total costs and those felt by public officials. As noted earlier, the parochial views of individual officials are often molded by the bargaining process into reasonably harmonious and beneficial patterns of action. Even pork-barrel spending may not be so bad when compared with realistic alternatives. It is a bad result of spillovers, of course, in comparison with some sort of ideal situation. Yet the pork barrel may be the price of having checks and balances (for example, of having congressmen from individual states and districts rather than from the United States at large), and these checks and balances are worth quite a price. To eliminate an externality completely would be like producing any product out to the point where its marginal worth was zero, and at this point one would almost certainly be using resources that have positive value to produce something having zero value. Some so-called "waste" is economical. To recover *all* the gold in a mining operation would cost more than it would be worth. To eliminate *all* wasteful expenditures that result from logrolling would sacrifice more than it would gain.

implications for the analysis of public spending

What significance does the unseen hand in government, and its imperfection, have for us? First of all, in thinking about public spending, one ought to keep in mind the existence of this invisible hand and the way it works. It tends to harness individual interests within government to carry out broader objectives. It keeps parochial viewpoints from yielding exclusively parochial policies. Second, however, one should keep in mind the imperfections of the mechanism—the fact that there are often major spillovers affecting parties who have inadequate voices in the bargaining process. Moreover, it should be recognized that many questionable policies or choices are inherent in the institutional framework and should not be blamed on bad officials or bad luck. Where the bargaining process does not eliminate or offset serious spillovers, the cost-reward structures confronting officials tend to pull them toward decisions that one may not like.

Third, it should be recognized that these imperfections do not mean that the absence of government activity would be better. One should not behave like the emperor who awarded the prize to the second singer immediately after hearing the first. Instead one should study the anatomy of market failure, the anatomy of government failure, and the possibilities of finding arrangements that he prefers.[27] Finally, with respect to whatever activities are in the public sector, an appreciation of the unseen hand is essential to the understanding of expenditure choices[28] and to the perception of possible improvements. Subsequent chapters, in attempts to explain spending choices, to see the effects of governmental decisions, or point the way to choices that one might prefer, will frequently hark back to the bargaining mechanism and ask, "What actions were, or would become, relatively expensive to various decision makers?"

---

[27] Others have stressed that none of the alternatives is perfect. For example, see Francis M. Bator's reminder that our real choice is among various inefficient arrangements (*The Question of Government Spending*, Harper & Row, Publishers, Incorporated, New York, 1960, pp. 99–112).

[28] For an excellent discussion of bargaining, not at the congressional level but by and among officials in the executive branch of government, see Richard E. Neustadt, *Presidential Power*, John Wiley & Sons, Inc., New York, 1960, especially pp. 33–57.

three

Chapter 2 described, in very general terms, how
public spending (and other) decisions *are* made.
Another fundamental matter is whether or not there
is any sound basis for saying what spending choices
ought to be made. Does economic efficiency serve
as a suitable criterion for reaching these decisions?
Can one identify in any ultimate sense the correct
public spending choices?

By using terms that are devoid of specific content, one can state a criterion. Efficient or correct
choices are those that yield the most gain or benefit
from available resources. One can also point out
that efficiency does not mean miserliness or cost
paring regardless of the gains that might be produced. Nor does it mean insistence on achieving
particular gains regardless of the cost (i.e., the sacrifice of other desirable things). One can add that
a familiar rule for deriving maximum benefits calls
for the production of each government good or
service out to the point at which the marginal cost
equals the marginal benefit. For any line of output,
this marginal gain is the worth of an extra unit of
output, and the marginal cost is the benefit foregone by producing the extra unit of that output,
that is, the value of alternative goods that could

have been produced. If the marginal benefit of education exceeds the marginal cost, total benefits can be increased by taking some resources from other activities and devoting them to education. If the marginal cost exceeds the marginal gains, total benefits can be expanded by taking some resources from education and devoting them to other activities.

Difficulties arise, however, when one tries to put content into the concept of "benefits" (and therefore into the concept of costs, which are simply alternative benefits foregone). An individual can have a utility function that is unambiguously correct *for him*. He can tell if *he* prefers A or B—that is, he can tell if A would yield more gains to him than B would. The concept of "benefits" is unambiguous in these circumstances. But public expenditures are group decisions. This is not to say there is some entity called a "group" that makes decisions; it merely means that government spending choices affect many persons. Compulsory taxation to establish a court system or to help the underprivileged affects more than one individual. Each person can identify the governmental choices that *he* would prefer, but there is no preference or utility function that is inherently correct for the group. All members may conceivably agree upon every choice or agree to abide by the results of majority rule, free markets in a specified framework, or delegation of all authority to certain persons. If one individual dissents, however, he may suffer in silence, attempt to persuade the others, or fight—but there is no "right" choice or ultimately correct group-preference function to be maximized.

That this is so will be made clear by a simple example: Imagine that three men are choosing a book to be read by all three (or deciding anything else that affects all three). If there is disagreement, should the criterion of the correct choice be the maximization of one man's utility, the maximization of one man's utility subject to constraints on the utility of others, decision by majority rule, the avoidance of violence, the maximization of aggregate utility (if individual utilities could be measured), or decision by voluntary exchange (which allows monetary "bribes" and enables each person to maximize his utility so long as he does not reduce another person's utility)? Logic does not compel one to prefer any of these outcomes—there is no ultimately correct way to measure or even conceive of benefits and no test of the fundamentally correct course of action.[1] What can be said, then, about criteria and efficiency?

---

[1] See also Kenneth J. Arrow, *Social Choice and Individual Values*, 2d ed., John Wiley & Sons, Inc., New York, 1963; G. C. Archibald, "The Qualitative Content of Maximizing Models," *Journal of Political Economy*, February, 1965, pp. 27–36; and James M. Buchanan and Gordon Tullock, *The Calculus of Consent*, The University of Michigan Press, Ann Arbor, Mich., 1962.

As might be expected, these points have special significance for Chapter 8, "Economic Calculus to Increase Efficiency."

efficiency in producing specified outputs

If members of a group agree regarding certain values, it is sometimes possible to identify a unique optimum or at least a set of superior points. If it is agreed, for example, to maximize the output of a specific product with given resources, this amounts to agreeing that only this product has value; and there is no ambiguity about the maximum. If it is agreed to maximize the number of identical *baskets* of products—each basket containing, for example, 2 pounds of rice, one 6-transistor radio, and five identical renditions of Beethoven's Ninth Symphony—there is no lack of clarity about the optimal position.

But complications arise when one wants to maximize "output" involving two or more products. At best one can only trace out a *set* of superior or efficient points (often called a production-possibility boundary) which shows the maximum Y that can be obtained for each amount of X that might be produced. At any point on this boundary, one cannot have more of one product without sacrificing some of the other. From any point inside the boundary, it *is* possible to have more of one without sacrificing any of another. Being on this boundary—that is, economic efficiency—can serve as a criterion for sorting out efficient from inefficient points. This criterion will not reveal which particular point is optimal, however.

In public spending decisions, unfortunately, the problems to be solved are not this simple. The choices are *not* intended to maximize one particular output, to maximize the number of identical baskets of products, or even to be on the production-possibility boundary in terms of *conventional* products. The attainable combinations of outputs are myriad; many data on inputs and outputs are inevitably expressed in monetary values; and unless there is full agreement, it is impossible to shelve questions about these values.

pareto optimality

One set of values that can be attached to commodities (material or nonmaterial) are values reflecting the substitution ratios that would emerge if unrestricted voluntary exchange were to occur. Why might this make sense? Whenever voluntary exchange takes place, with no third parties affected involuntarily, at least one person is made better off, as *he* sees *his* well-being, and nobody is made worse off, as *each one* sees *his* well-being. If certain conditions prevail and the process continues until no one can make himself better off without making someone else worse off (as each perceives his own well-being), the situation is called "Pareto optimality,"[2] and it has considerable appeal as a

---

[2] So called after Vilfredo Pareto (1848–1923), the Italian economist and sociologist to whom the concept is attributed.

criterion for sorting out a set of preferred situations from less desirable positions. (If Pareto optimality existed, the economy would have to be somewhere on the production-possibility boundary in terms of products, and for some purposes one might regard economic efficiency and Pareto optimality as being synonymous.)

When Pareto optimality is used as a criterion, the accompanying substitution ratios or prices become in effect the values attached to the outputs. What is so sacred about these measures of value? Nothing is sacred about them, and indeed these prices, and the combination of goods produced, would change with a shift in the initial distribution of wealth among individuals. The rationale for using these prices to measure benefits is simply that (in the right circumstances) they lead to Pareto optimality; if one likes Pareto optimality as a partial criterion, he presumably likes the use of such prices. Incidentally, they would reflect the values that every user, in whatever particular circumstances prevailed, attached to an item. Sometimes people doubt this, believing that Mr. X might be willing to offer $100 for another dozen oranges and Mr. Y might be willing to pay only 5 cents, while the price might be $1 per dozen. If people have unrestricted access to markets, however, Mr. X would buy more oranges until another dozen was worth no more to him than the price, and Mr. Y would sell or cease buying oranges until the last dozen bought was worth the price. The price then, approximately measures the marginal worth of the output to each and every person who buys it at all.

Despite its appealing features, though, Pareto optimality is by no means a satisfactory criterion. For one thing, as already noted, it does a rather rough job of sorting, for it merely segregates one infinite set of Pareto-optimal points from another infinite set of other points. For finer sorting, additional value judgments about wealth distribution have to be made, and it is highly improbable that members of a group can agree on these judgments. (Also, as will be noted later, people often seem to prefer indirect rather than direct means of redistributing wealth.) This is one reason why Pareto optimality is no ultimate test of "correct" group action.

For another thing, one cannot find *clear-cut* guidance even to the set of Pareto-optimal positions, and therefore personal judgments inevitably enter into policy preferences. In real life unrestricted voluntary exchange—full side payments to take advantage of *all* mutually advantageous trades—does not occur.[3] The conditions for achieving such optimality are so stringent, the costs of

---

[3] Buchanan and Tullock have pointed out that full side payments would lead to a point *somewhere* on the Pareto-optimal boundary (*ibid.*, pp. 186–188). One has to conclude, though, that in actuality heavy transaction costs and other barriers prevent many such trades. (Or he might conclude that whenever violence is not occurring, the economy is *always* somewhere on the boundary.)

many actions so hard to see, that this criterion can rarely point the way plainly. In the private sector, for example, there are many deviations from the conditions for Pareto optimality and many situations in which the rules do not reveal what remedial government actions, if any, would lead toward this optimality. As noted in Chapter 2, there are externalities—interdependencies that are not taken into account by contractual arrangements. There are departures from competition. There are legal or other constraints on entry into occupations or on the consideration of substitution possibilities, constraints that may or may not be economical to change. Many persons would say that some kinds of advertising are wasteful. Utility functions are interdependent—that is, to some extent what Jones buys affects my satisfaction—and making Jones better off may automatically make me worse off. (With interdependent utility functions there would still be a set of points where no one could be made better off without making someone worse off, but these would no longer be points on the outermost production-possibility boundary.)

In many of these circumstances, the question of government intervention arises. But the costs of doing something about externalities, oligopoly, price distortions, and other departures from the ideal are hard to discern, particularly in a world of changing tastes and technology. If one applies rules for achieving Pareto optimality mechanically and incorrectly, he may find himself trying to increase efficiency regardless of cost![4] To force people to draw up contracts or take other action to "internalize" externalities may cost more than it would gain.[5] To charge direct marginal cost when this would not cover total cost may divorce subsequent output and investment decisions from consumers' evaluations. That is, since this policy prevents covering total costs or discovering what mix of outputs would maximize profits, it prevents one from learning whether or not consumers prefer a different mix of outputs or a different amount invested in the enterprise involved. The result is a sacrifice of valuable information, a component cost that is hard to measure, since special markets for this information are not viable. In these circumstances too, what action (if any) could benefit some persons without harming others is not clear.

Furthermore, since all the conditions for optimality are not fulfilled, one cannot be sure that rules for meeting part of the conditions will truly lead to improvements. This point has most frequently been made in what is called the

---

[4] See William J. Baumol and Richard E. Quandt, "Rules of Thumb and Optimally Imperfect Decisions," *American Economic Review*, March, 1964, pp. 23–46; James M. Buchanan, "Politics, Policy, and the Pigovian Margins," *Economica*, February, 1962, pp. 17–19; and Roland N. McKean and Jora R. Minasian, "On Achieving Pareto Optimality—Regardless of Cost!" *Western Economic Journal*, Fall, 1966.

[5] Harold Demsetz, "The Exchange and Enforcement of Property Rights," *Journal of Law and Economics*, October, 1964, pp. 11–26.

"theory of second best,"[6] though the term is something of a misnomer, since it is the theory of the attainable first best that is in trouble. Whether it is called first or second best, all individuals are groping for the best they can do, given various constraints. This is an imperfect world, and the constraints are so complex that it is often difficult to perceive what is the best that one can do. That is about what the theory of second best says. In any event there are troublesome issues. For example, if one "suboptimizes" and looks only at production by one monopolist, one may conclude that price should be made equal to marginal cost. If one looks at a whole economy containing *numerous* monopolists with *diverse* ratios of output prices to marginal costs, it is hard to see what government price policy would bring gains in excess of costs.

These difficulties have usually been discussed with reference to the private sector; but in the public sector too these same troubles handicap one in using Pareto optimality as a criterion. The governmental counterpart of monopoly is pervasive. Agencies with strong bargaining power tend to adopt distorted price-output policies. Furthermore, even if a project appears to be economic from the standpoint of total costs and benefits in several states, one state may refuse to bargain, hoping for a "free ride." The establishment of new government agencies to support innovations and to supplant obsolete practices or products is surely more difficult than the entry of new companies into the private sector. As was shown in Chapter 2, externalities in government are pervasive. Economical bargaining or contractual arrangements to internalize them are harder to achieve in the public sector than in the private economy (witness the fact that political processes make possible only a relatively limited amount of bargaining).

Institutional constraints on the consideration of substitution possibilities are, if anything, more prominent in government than in the private sphere. In the absence of adequate competitive forces, Congress must control what is done with the funds it appropriates by prohibiting the executive branch from making significant shifts of resources from one category to another without reprogramming permission. The executive departments in turn "shred out" subcategories of expenditure and discourage resource shifts among them. Moreover, legislators and officials, having only twenty-four hours in the day, frown on reprogramming requests from below. In other words, in government there are numerous institutional barriers to the consideration of substitution possibilities. As usual, the existence of such constraints or rules of thumb may bring more gain than cost, but without markets for the various consequences it is hard to tell.

---

[6] The article that brought this topic to the fore was R. G. Lipsey and K. Lancaster, "The General Theory of Second Best," *Review of Economic Studies*, vol. 24 (1956–1957), pp. 11–32.

The other difficulties described above with reference to the public sector are also present in the public sphere. There is the counterpart of advertising, which some would consider wasteful, as each agency tries to get and keep a clientele. Utility functions are interdependent in both the private economy and the government sector: in either sphere, what Jones does and gets may affect my satisfaction. To charge direct marginal cost for the use of a public park might, as might such a charge in the private sector, divorce subsequent output and investment choices from consumers' demands and entail an additional hard-to-measure cost. Because of these imperfections, the theory of second best is just as disturbing with respect to the government sector or the whole economy as it is with respect to the market sector (see the later section on "suboptimization"). With regard to all these shortcomings in both the private and public sector, the question of public action cannot be avoided—unless one is willing to say, "Well, given whatever action or inaction the government adopts, voluntary exchange will then do the best it can and lead the economy to *some* Pareto-optimal position." If one says that, however, the criterion does not enable one to distinguish any point from any other point. Thus, Pareto optimality fails to give precise guidance about either public regulation of the private sector or about other public-expenditure choices. As a result, personal judgments must play major roles in policy selection.

A matter that deserves special emphasis when trying to define efficiency is the pervasiveness of uncertainty. At best, each cost and gain is a probability distribution of possible magnitudes, not a unique impact. Each point on the Pareto-optimal boundary is really a family of points, different probabilities being associated with each point. The set of relationships that the positive sciences have tested and in which we can have confidence is not complete. One cannot predict even the physical consequences of actions with certainty. There are still areas of doubt in physics and chemistry. The direct and the side effects of drugs used to treat tuberculosis, the fertility of various soils when irrigated, the implications of automobile travel for smog and noise levels—such physical relationships are still not known with a high degree of confidence.

When one turns to the social sciences, ignorance is still more impressive. Hypotheses that have been subjected to satisfactory checks in sociology, economics, psychology, and political science are relatively scarce. There are many untested models but few tested ones. One cannot predict with any assurance the impact of a particular housing program on crime rates or family stability or group antagonisms, of a particular educational proposal on juvenile delinquency, of a particular institutional arrangement on the behavior of government officials, or even of a specific deficit on aggregate demand.

Analogous uncertainties must be faced in businesses and households as well as in government. In his personal life, in order to make better choices, a man spends a large portion of his time and energy getting information, deciding how much information to get, and deciding how probable it is that various propositions are correct. In the business world, the purpose of an enormous number of ventures is to seek or provide information—witness employment exchanges, advertising agencies, newspapers, consumers' research organizations, private investigators, talent-search agencies, mailing-list services, aptitude-testing agencies, publishers of catalogs and directories, and so on. Labeling activities are to a considerable extent in the business of conveying information, always, of course, in terms of probabilities. A Grade A stamp on eggs or meat, an electrician's license, membership in an association, a high-school certificate, a Phi Beta Kappa key, a prison record—all these labels serve partly to convey information; i.e., the probability is relatively high that items in each set have certain characteristics. No employer, colleague, neighbor, government official, or other person has a crystal ball. Each person must make choices on the basis of fragments of imperfect information. (Employers may care less about what a business-administration graduate with good grades has learned than they care about the information conveyed by his degree—namely that, as a member of the set of persons with business-administration degrees, the graduate *probably* has above-average ability, is interested in business, and is industrious.)

As a result of such uncertainties, one must make personal judgments about the physical and sociological consequences of government actions. But he must also make personal judgments about the utility or worth of those consequences. Suppose two steps to prevent accidents would entail the same resource-costs: Step A would save one-hundred lives, while Step B has a 0.5 probability of saving ten lives and a 0.5 probability of saving two-hundred lives. Which course of action produces the greater gain from specified resources? The answer depends upon an individual's utility function and will vary from one person to the next. Each must make a judgment about the utility of different probability distributions. This suggests that acquiring more information to reduce uncertainties, or designing a modified policy to hedge against poorer outcomes, may be worth the cost. As a consequence, activities that appear superficially to be wasteful, such as waiting, holding assets idle, or trial-and-error probing, merit consideration. But the implication for the present argument is that there is no clear-cut criterion of economic efficiency in such conditions.

Thus far it has been pointed out that Pareto optimality (1) points, at best, to an infinite set of points rather than to a unique position and (2) cannot give precise guidance because personal judgments have to be made about the costs and gains from many actions.

Third on the list of general difficulties with Pareto optimality is the basic fact that, while it has considerable appeal, there is no compelling reason for one to accept Pareto optimality as a criterion at all. It is not true that achievement of this kind of efficiency maximizes total satisfaction, for some people may be veritable satisfaction machines, while others are dull clods. For that matter it is not clear that one would wish to maximize *total* satisfaction, even if it could be measured. Would a person sleep any better at night if he could say, "Because we give most of the world's wealth to people who know how to live it up, I know that *total* satisfaction in the world is being maximized." Nor is it clear that achieving Pareto optimality maximizes any other magnitude that it is indubitably desirable to maximize.

There is nothing illogical about my *not* wanting individual X to maximize his utility as *he* sees it. I may feel that his heavy consumption of calories or of nightclub entertainment is unwise or immoral and should be restricted. You may think this is intolerant of me, but it may nonetheless be part of my preference (utility) function. I may wish to take actions or have actions taken without buying the consent of individuals who find those actions objectionable. I may therefore prefer to deviate from Pareto optimality (in its conventional sense)[7] as a criterion, and so may a majority of voters. Indeed if people are candid, they will admit that economic efficiency in this sense is no one's first choice; for each would prefer to distribute wealth, encourage the use of some products, and discourage the consumption of others, according to his own fancy. (Since most individuals have little chance of doing these things, however, they may generally prefer, as second best, to tolerate individual choices rather than to try to control all choices themselves. If A claims to know what is good for others, the others can just as legitimately claim to know what is good for A.) In other words, individuals may attach values to specific constraints or rules that prevent the achievement of economic efficiency in its usual sense. As Schumpeter put it, one may prefer socialist (or capitalist) bread, even if it has mice in it.

In government, certainly, the unseen hand results in officials' giving weight to many values that would not emerge in voluntary exchange. For example, officials may attach greater value to additional economic growth than is implied by individual choices. They may attach high values to self-sufficiency, family-size farms, cohesiveness or discipline, or national prestige, and these values may be sanctioned by a majority of the voters. In addition, even with democratic procedures, officials end up with some discretionary authority, and they are likely to introduce additional aims that may or may not be condoned by controlling coalitions of voters. For instance, a value may be attached to having

---

[7] There would still exist a production-possibility boundary given the resulting constraints, but it would not be what is usually meant by the set of Pareto-optimal points.

relatives on the payroll, carrying out pet schemes, subsidizing particular religions, developing Death Valley, controlling certain prices, forbidding certain side agreements, or having more personal convenience. There is nothing wrong or right about these values any more than there is anything wrong or right about a taste for oranges or castor oil. One may regard these preferences as introducing constraints that prevent the attainment of the usual production-possibility boundary or alter the particular point that is attained. Or one could view them as introducing new "products" that are valued and require resources to produce but are in effect omitted from conventional production possibilities —new products that therefore change the nature of the boundary.

➤ If people could agree to accept Pareto optimality as a goal—or, in other words, agree to accept the results of unrestricted voluntary exchange as a goal— it might be a relatively desirable way to resolve conflicts. The alternative ways of settling conflicting demands appear to be various mixes of (1) rules or traditions, (2) the blackmail variety of persuasion, and (3) force. But these alternatives tend to result in dominance by a few. Many issues will always be settled by these means, of course; but the degree to which an economy relies on them is subject to modification.

Some political economists have tried to expore what might be called "voting optimality"—that is, the conditions for bargaining and voting procedures to lead to optimal choices.[8] In Chapter 2, "The Unseen Hand in Government," some implications of the bargaining mechanism were discussed. One may be able to conceive of a community with voting rights as divisible and exchangeable as money: such a community would reach something like Pareto optimality by voting. In any event, agreeing to abide by decisions reached in a framework including a Bill of Rights and numerous checks and balances has some of the virtue of a voluntary exchange process: as long as agreement to abide by the rules persists, it resolves conflicts in a peaceful way while still permitting some diversity in views. Not much is really known, however, about alternative sets of checks and balances and their implications. About all one can say thus far is that some vote trading is better than no vote trading, that some bargaining within government is better than no bargaining (but one can hardly imagine such an extreme), that unanimously favored proposals are steps in the right direction, and that in certain circumstances, vote trading could lead to such steps.

To sum up: In appraising spending or other government choices, people

---

[8] E. A. Thompson, "A Pareto Optimal Group Decision Process," in Gordon Tullock (ed.), *Papers on Non-market Decision Making*, Thomas Jefferson Center for Political Economy, Charlottesville, Va., 1966. On all these matters, see especially the fascinating work of Buchanan and Tullock, *op. cit.*

must make personal judgments. Since the positive sciences cannot predict all the effects of an action with certainty, people must inject personal judgments about those effects on the basis of whatever clues are available. Since values are debatable, they must also make personal value judgments. People can legitimately disagree, therefore, and there is no criterion that can point to the correct public spending choices. Just as physical efficiency (e.g., percentage of heat units converted into usable energy by a steam engine) is an inadequate guide to choice because it ignores value and cost, so economic efficiency is an inadequate guide to choice because it can neglect *elements* of value and cost.

suboptimization and the theory of first best

As noted above, the theory of second best, or in other words the theory of attainable first best, presents difficulties in the public sector as well as in the private sector. In making any spending choice, one faces an uncertain and complicated network of constraints. The matter is sufficiently important in government to warrant this special discussion.

These constraints stem in part from the fact that information, analysis, and decision making are themselves expensive. It costs something to ignore alternatives, but it also costs something to explore alternatives. To examine all options simultaneously is prohibitively expensive, indeed impossible. So people break the overall economic problem down into "subproblems." They do the best they can to solve these subproblems of choice by making what are sometimes called "suboptimizations": they compare the costs and benefits of the alternatives that are factored out as the subproblem of choice. People also do the best they can to slice off, or factor out, subproblems economically. This means comparing the cost of including a larger or smaller set of alternatives in the suboptimization with the gains from doing so.

Where it appears to be preferable, one encourages markets and contractual arrangements and delegates certain subproblems to firms and other private organizations. Within the public sector, particular subproblems of choice are delegated to different levels of government and, within the Federal government, to different levels of officialdom. In the analysis of particular choices, where the costs of examining other alternatives simultaneously appear to be too high, one shelves those other choices temporarily and neglects the possible interdependencies. Where the costs of additional information about alternatives seems likely to exceed the gains from the extra information, one reaches decisions without it.

The way the overall economic problem is broken into smaller problems is suggested by Figure 1. This process of breaking out subproblems for analysis or for delegation to lower-level authorities poses some danger of inefficiency. It may mean that certain trade-offs—certain sets of alternatives—will be overlooked. For example, it may be that *no* official will really be responsible for comparing the marginal worth of programs to prevent tuberculosis with that of programs to protect the health of Army personnel (since these activities are in different departments). If analysts try to assess the marginal worth of health programs in various departments, they still will not be able to consider *all* possible alternatives.

One option that it is particularly important not to neglect is the use of resources to invent new alternatives. In the public as well as the private sector, technological advance and the design of new alternatives, that is, pushing the production-possibility curve outward, can be fully as important as approaching the existing boundary by careful calculation. Efficiency does not call for one to choose the best alternative from a bad lot—that is, to ignore the utility of a search for better options.[9]

Dealing with suboptimizations may also fail to reveal interdependencies or spillover effects. A government agency is responsible for its assigned activities and is likely to be less keenly aware of the impacts of its actions on other agencies than of the impacts on its own activities. Anyone responsible for flood-control works is more likely to ask what his actions can do for flood control than what he can do for overall efficiency. Anyone selecting among alternative police vehicles will overlook relevant consequences unless he fits the vehicles into the larger crime-deterrent function to see what would be the impacts of their speed, reliability, conspicuousness, and cost on the effectiveness of the entire police, welfare, and perhaps law-court budgets.

But note that exploring additional alternatives, searching for information, designing innovations, or trying to trace out more interdependencies all involve costs. One should not proceed in any of these directions regardless of sacrifice. In making up his mind, an individual should not factor out subproblems, neglect alternatives, ignore spillovers, or use crude criteria—if he has reason to believe that these actions would cost more than they would gain. Nor should he turn to higher-level optimizations, try to examine a longer list of alternatives, try to trace out more interdependencies, or seek less imperfect criteria—if such actions would cost more than they would gain. And these costs and gains are exceedingly difficult to measure or even to discern. As stressed before, these and related considerations mean that personal judgments must be made, and there is no clear-cut guide to the attainable first best.

---

[9] Harvey Leibenstein, "Allocative Efficiency Vs. 'X-Efficiency,'" *American Economic Review*, June, 1966, pp. 392–415.

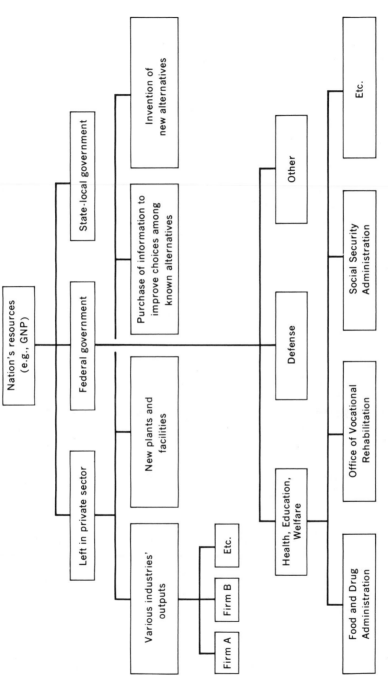

FIG. 1 The economic problem (resource allocation) as a multitude of "subproblems" of choice

what can be said about public spending?

If no particular policy or set of policies is correct from the standpoint of the group, what can usefully be said about public spending choices? Several things can be said that may help each individual decide what policies *he* prefers. Also, *if* there is sufficient consensus regarding preferences, these points may contribute to the adoption of policies that are generally desirable. Then, too, apart from public policy, the study of the economics of public spending, like the study of any positive science, may advance our understanding of the world. Such studies may have long-run values that cannot now be perceived.

One of the useful things that can be done is to emphasize general principles of choosing. These principles give no specific guidance concerning policy selection, but they do offer guidance in thinking about choices. One such principle is that one should compare alternatives, not blindly pursue some unique benefit or requirement or need regardless of the sacrifice entailed. Even by itself, an understanding of this principle is a significant step forward, because most of us are strongly tempted to distill from our good intentions a belief in unique needs. For instance, if the rat population in a city is such that occupants of houses each encounter five rats per month, this is deplorable, and one instinctively feels that this phenomenon must be eliminated. Yet in fact the action one advocates should depend upon its cost and upon what the costs and gains from *alternative* steps would be. A host of other possible actions should be considered—perhaps lower standards than the complete elimination of the rates (say, reducing the encounters to two per month) and higher standards (such as eliminating the rats plus otherwise improving the houses). Almost never are there unique needs; with altered costs or gains, the actions, spending decisions, or quantities of items that are needed change. In making up his mind about a public expenditure decision, each individual should recognize this fact.

Another principle that will come up from time to time is that the existence of something wrong—even hideously wrong—in one situation does not mean that a proposed change would automatically be better. My favorite illustration of this point is the remark sometimes attributed to Maurice Chevalier: When asked how he felt about growing older, he is said to have replied, "Well, there are many things wrong with it, but it's better than the alternative." This is a remarkable planet, and yet—with pestilence, tidal waves, and three billion individuals on it—one has no natural right to expect a society that is free of misery, oppression, violence, and horror. One always has to seek the best *attainable* alternative.

Another general principle is that when a policy has uncertain effects, its worth to an individual is the utility of those uncertain effects—not the utility of spuriously specific consequences. To be sure, it is often economical to use rules of thumb in evaluating public policies; but it is all too common, it seems to me, for individuals to consider thoroughly distorted pictures of policies' effects—one major distortion being a gross neglect of inherent uncertainties. Many persons seem to convince themselves that they know with certainty the effects of public housing, of escalating a war or of withdrawing, of permitting or not permitting riots.

Aside from general principles, one can trace out part of the effects of alternative policies much as consumers' research sketches out the consequences to consumers of purchasing alternative automobiles, and this can help individuals decide what they prefer. Although mentioned earlier, this is really the contribution of all science and analysis to public-policy formation, and it deserves further emphasis. Like chemistry or physics, economics can develop hypotheses, test them, establish relationships or "laws," and make improved predictions of the consequences of alternative government actions. Then, without preattachment of value tags to any of these consequences, one can better identify the policy he prefers. For example, one can better choose his position on nuclear weapons if he can predict their thermal effects; on air pollution if he understands the impacts of exhaust gases; on a zero price for water if he knows what the response of farmers will be. Similarly, knowing more about the effects of smoking on the incidence of cancer does not reveal what any individual *should* do, but the knowledge can help him identify his preferred course of action. Unfortunately, the testing of hypotheses in the social sciences proceeds slowly, and in this study no propositions are tested, though it is hoped that some new ones are at least suggested.

A final set of things that can be said about public spending includes discussions of the consequences of alternative policies in which prices and value judgments *are* deliberately introduced. For example, the pricing of public goods, the use of cost-benefit analyses, and other issues will be discussed, part of the time with Pareto optimality resurrected as a partial criterion. These discussions and analyses, too, are like consumers' research, for they trace out consequences of alternative policies that may be relevant to some, though not to all, individuals' choices. If the implied values are accepted, the guidance or analyses will be relevant. To persons who do not accept the same values, they will presumably be unhelpful.

In the remaining chapters, these arguments about criteria should be kept in mind. The materials should be regarded as attempts to contribute to our understanding and, after the fashion of consumers' research, to aid individuals in deciding what policies or positions they prefer. But no particular policy or position—either conservative or liberal—is demonstrably correct from the standpoint of all individuals. No science—not even economics—can say with finality what *ought* to be done in public spending.

part
two

SOME EFFECTS OF PUBLIC OUTLAYS

One major effect (and aim) of government spending is to influence the distribution of wealth among individuals. Taxes and expenditures inevitably reduce the wealth of some and increase that of others. This is not to say that anyone would favor or disfavor a government program solely because of its distributional implications. There is always a multiplicity of considerations. Like alternative jobs or automobiles, alternative government programs have a variety of characteristics or attributes that are relevant to one's choice. Indeed the purchase of tangible items like irrigation projects and the purchase of transfer programs like payments to veterans are not as dissimilar as is sometimes suggested. At least, the way individuals choose among such proposals is similar; in deciding about both purchases, individuals seek preferred combinations of utilities that can be called "goods."

It is virtually impossible to find any spending measures that are purely transfers or that affect only the allocation of resources. Most spending decisions involve both of these effects and others that influence individuals' utilities. It is doubtful that anyone concludes, "I support this program because it would allocate U.S. resources more efficiently," or "I choose this program because it redistributes wealth in the way I deem to be desirable." This would be similar to saying, "I choose Brand X bread because of the taste," disregarding the packaging, location, freshness, and all other considerations. Each government outlay, like each private expenditure, is for a package of attributes; and the individuals involved seek to maximize utility, that is, to select preferred packages—not simply to buy according to a public-goods principle or an equity principle (or, in selecting our tax structure, simply to choose taxes according to a "benefit" principle or an ability-to-pay principle).

Why discuss these impacts of public spending separately, then? Partly because it is traditional to distinguish between transfers and purchases of goods and services, and partly because it *is* relatively useful to focus attention on these "ultimate products" of government spending, even if each activity produces several of them as joint effects.[1] To focus attention on the redistribution of wealth, one can sort out, in a loose fashion, choices whose *principal* impact is on wealth distribution or a major aim of which is to affect distribution.

Such choices are those pertaining to "transfer expenditures." The basis for sorting out these outlays is that the payments are not in exchange for tangible or marketable goods and services. As a consequence, the measurement of gains and losses is somewhat different for transfers from the way it is for government purchases of goods. The main point is that transfer payments are "nonexhaustive," meaning that a million-dollar transfer does not represent a using up of resources valued at $1 million. Adopting a transfer program such as relief payments does use up *some* resources, does cause us to forego alternatives (e.g., an alternative set of transfer payments), and implies a variety of costs and gains, but the amount spent does not convey much information about the size of the net resource cost. On exhaustive expenditures, on the other hand, the amount spent does indicate reasonably well the value of steel, cement, man-hours, land, and so on that are used up by purchasing the goods and services.[2]

Restricted grants and subsidies are in a sense hybrids, for to some extent they purchase specific tangible goods. For instance, Medicare payments will really purchase and provide medical treatment and services just as though the government bought these items directly and distributed them. In part, however—and this would also be true of providing recreation services or anything else below cost—the services substitute for consumer purchases that would

---

[1] For example, Richard A. Musgrave discusses allocation, distribution, and stabilization as major "products" of government activities (in his *Theory of Public Finance: A Study in Public Economy*, McGraw-Hill Book Company, New York, 1959, pp. 3–27ff.).

[2] Provided one accepts the marginal evaluations of individual consumers in the existing market situation as being the appropriate measure of resource values.

For more on exhaustive versus nonexhaustive expenditures, see Francis M. Bator, *The Question of Government Spending*, Harper & Row, Publishers, Incorporated, New York, 1960, pp. 9–39; and Musgrave, *op. cit.*, pp. 191–193.

have been made anyway, and in effect the payments transfer purchasing power to the recipients. This underscores once more the difficulties of drawing a significant hard-and-fast line between transfers and purchases of goods and services. In a technical sense, however, the line is clear. Transfer payments are not *direct* purchases of tangible goods and services.

Decisions that have comparatively large effects on wealth distribution, that is, transfer expenditures, will be examined first, and those having relatively large direct impacts on resource allocation will be discussed in Chapter 5. Transfers are given priority here because they appear to be of growing significance. Issues about redistribution seem likely to play a key role in shaping government expenditures and the nature of the society.[3] As noted in Chapter 1, transfer expenditures have already become quite large, and the legislation that has been passed during President Johnson's administration suggests that continued growth is likely. For the fiscal year 1966, estimated transfer payments by the U.S. Federal government amount to $35.2 billion, and grants-in-aid to state and local governments amount to $13 billion. In the future, the totals seem likely to be much higher, especially because of the growth of old-age and retirement benefits, transfers in connection with the "war on poverty," payments to veterans, grants-in-aid to lower-level governmental units (see Chapter 10), subsidies to occupants of public housing, disbursements under the Medicare program, payments to the unemployed, and subsidies of other sorts.

utility maximization and transfer expenditures

How do individual voters, officials, and politicians decide what positions to take regarding proposed (or existing) transfer programs? Each person tries to decide which course of action he prefers—after appraising the alternatives in the only way he can: through his own mind and senses and in view of all rather than part of the elements affecting his utility. Students are sometimes told that one should approve of or disapprove of outlays for goods and services on the basis of economic efficiency, but that one should make up his mind about transfers on the basis of equity considerations. As mentioned earlier, it is doubtful that anyone uses his conception of equity as his sole criterion. He does not ask, "Would this program be a step toward the distribution of wealth that I regard as fair?" To repeat, individuals reach decisions about transfers as well as the

---

[3] Wealth distribution might be an issue of growing importance if automation and population growth lowered the marginal productivity of unskilled labor relative to the marginal productivity of capital. For reflections on this possibility and on the merits of alternative ways of redistributing wealth, see James E. Meade, *Efficiency, Equality, and Ownership of Property*, George Allen & Unwin, Ltd., London, 1964.

production of defense capabilities in the light of impacts on a long list of elements in their utility functions. Then when one specifies some of these elements in people's utility functions and recalls that demand curves have negative slopes, one can better understand, and perhaps predict, the shaping of transfer programs; for the more expensive an increment in one element of utility (or in a particular policy) becomes to an individual, the less of it he will want.

possible gains in utility to the individual

Let us try to specify a few of the elements of utility functions that may be affected by transfer programs. Suppose you are asking yourself whether or not you favor a proposed program, say higher payments to the poverty-stricken or unemployed. What are some things that might be affected so as to increase your utility?

(1) One consideration would indeed be whether or not the proposal would earn points in terms of your ethical judgments. If the program would, in your view, lead to a more equitable distribution of wealth, this effect of the program would yield some gain in utility to you and would be one factor tending to induce you to approve the proposal. You might feel strongly about this consideration because wealth distribution in an exchange society does not seem particularly fair. Individuals tend to be rewarded according to the marginal productivity of various skills and assets, and this depends on many variables other than initiative and hard work. To acquire wealth, one should select wisely not only his parents and home background, but also his genes and chromosomes. Or consider women's differing marginal productivities in "marrying well": women who lack diligence and admirable character (or whatever features one regards as meritorious) often wear mink coats, while many "deserving" wives who married less well struggle to exist and rear their children. Marginal productivity is greatly enhanced if one has a skill for which the demand soars, and completely unforeseeable events have much to do with this. Finally, a good way to end up with a small fortune is to start out with a big one. The result is not indisputably a fair distribution of wealth. It should be emphasized, however, that no other distribution is indisputably fair either; shifts in any direction are likely to bring minus as well as plus utilities to an individual, and he must weigh these against each other to see what shifts he prefers.

(2) Another highly relevant consideration would be the direct benefits, if any, that you might receive. If you happen to be a potential beneficiary, the program will be more appealing to you than it would otherwise be, even if the net impact on wealth distribution does not seem particularly equitable to you. The benefits could be in the form of receiving transfer payments or increases

in the value of your properties or stocks. (Medicare, for example, raised the value of certain businesses and corporation stocks.) The prospect of such gains means that the program would be relatively rewarding to you, or, to look at the other side of the coin, the absence of the program would be relatively expensive to you.

(3) Another factor that might well figure in your calculus would be any possible reduction in the probability of violence or the breakdown of law and order. If a particular group was so dissatisfied and restless that it posed a threat of violence, you might believe that the transfers would alleviate this threat, whether or not you regarded the result as being equitable. Even apart from any impact on your personal security, you could look upon law and order as a public good (a valuable aspect of the environment whose benefits can be consumed by some without rendering them unavailable to others). On the other hand, as noted in the next section, you might regard appeasement or yielding to "blackmail" as an action that would increase the subsequent threat to an orderly society. A squeaking wheel often gets some grease—unless it threatens to cause a complete breakdown, in which case the wheel is discarded. (4) A related consideration might be the maintenance of the existing decision-making rule. You might fear that, without the transfer program, the going system of checks and balances would be changed in an uncertain manner or in a manner that you would dislike. You might therefore attach positive value to a reduction in the probability of such rule changes and to a transfer program which you believed would lower that probability.

(5) You might also gain utility from the transfer program because you believed it would help free you and others from the nagging sense of responsibility for older, handicapped, or unemployed members of the family. You might also believe there would be advantages from the enhanced mobility of such a society. (6) Another gain from your approving of the program might be your gain in approval and support from your friends and associates—if they strongly endorsed the program. If you happened to be a politician or government official, this sort of factor (votes or support in bargaining for other objectives) would be a dominant consideration.

(7) You might feel that the transfer program would, at least in certain respects, improve incentives to work or invest or increase efficiency. For example, if members of a group feel that their situation is hopeless, they have little incentive to work or invest or increase their efficiency. If these persons can be given more hope—if they can be shown that increased effort does bring increased reward—one effect is likely to be heightened incentives, which can in turn make many persons better off. Some types of transfer programs might have this effect, which could have positive utility from your standpoint. (8) Yet another utility-conveying feature of a transfer program might be the likelihood

of a desirable shift in resource allocation. Most transfer programs shift some wealth in kind or induce recipients to purchase more of particular goods, such as medical care, education, and training, at the same time that they shift some generalized purchasing power. The result might be a gain from your standpoint because you believe that consumption of these items is ethically good, or that you know what is good for the recipients better than they do, or that there will be valuable bounce-back effects on you.

(9) You might also gain utility if the transfers would improve the lot of a particular group, such as veterans or nurses, to whom you felt some special sort of obligation or sympathy, even if the change did not strike you as being a step toward a generally equitable distribution of wealth. You can wish to pay someone a debt or give someone a gift even if you do not believe the action promotes an equitable distribution of wealth. (10) Still another gain might be the utility of honoring an explicit or implicit promise. Interest payments are usually regarded as transfers (though they could also be looked upon as payments for services) and these payments are stipulated in explicit contracts. A broken promise entails disutilities because of both moral and other considerations; a kept promise therefore brings gains in utility. (11) You might also benefit because of ideological reasons, i.e., because of your general beliefs apart from any of the preceding factors.

possible losses in utility to the individual

The possible gains in utility indicated above do not constitute an exhaustive list by any means, but they may suggest how numerous the elements of your preference function are. Similarly there are many elements that figure in utilities forgone or losses of preferredness. (1) The most obvious feature of a transfer program that would bring disutility to you is your anticipated share of the cost. Whether the program was financed by the income tax, excise taxes, the sale of bonds to banks, or the printing of money, you would probably end up bearing part of the burden. The size of your share of the cost would depend on many circumstances and would be highly uncertain,[4] but your judgment about this matter would have a bearing on whether or not you approved the transfer proposal. If you anticipated incurring a relatively large cost, having the gains from the program would be relatively expensive to you, and you would favor the program less than you would if you were to bear a smaller amount of cost.

As stressed before, you may deem it not worthwhile to find out much about this cost (or the other considerations), especially if you doubt that your posi-

---

[4] James M. Buchanan has explored this subject in his careful and extremely interesting study, *Public Finance in Democratic Process: Fiscal Institutions and Individual Choice*, University of North Carolina Press, Chapel Hill, N.C., 1967.

tion would have any effect on policy selection. In a British survey, over one-third of the respondents thought the National Health Service fully covered its expenses through NHS contributions, apparently unaware of the fact that tax-payers were paying 80 percent of the bill.[5] The evidence also suggested a remarkable lack of cost awareness in connection with the public pension system. Moreover, when people do acquire more accurate information, they presumably guess at their individual shares on the basis of exceedingly crude rules of thumb.

(2) Another forgone utility might be the benefits from an alternative program that would have to be given up. Or since you would be taking a position only on this one proposal, this disutility might take the form of a lowered probability of later getting some program that you would prefer. (3) Another cost to you might be a loss of flexibility or options entailed by the particular program. The Social Security program is set up, for instance, so that in many circumstances there is no alternative to having the coverage. Even if it appears to be a good thing from your standpoint, you may still lose some satisfaction because it reduces your or other persons' options. Buchanan has pointed this out with respect to the tax side; an individual may prefer excise taxes to personal income taxes (or to a lump-sum tax) because in a pinch the option of reducing his burden by avoiding the taxed items can be exercised more easily under the former.[6]

(4) You might suffer a little extra loss of utility if you recognized that in some respects the program would inflict real costs, instead of nonexhaustive transfers, on the economy. Included would be administrative costs in connection with both the taxes and disbursements and also the "unneutral effects" of the taxes, that is, the induced resource reallocations that would yield a lower level of wealth to various persons. These costs might cause you additional disutility because, like the loss of farm crops or anything else, the reduction in wealth could trickle down and around (by affecting various marginal productivities) until it ultimately reduced your own wealth and that of your neighbors. On grounds of economic efficiency as usually conceived, direct redistribution by means of lump-sum taxes and lump-sum transfers would be preferable to transfers involving unneutral effects. As noted earlier, however, some individuals may attach values to the unneutral effects themselves or to laws and regulations that produce them.

(5) A particularly important unneutral effect could come from any losses in incentives to work, invest, or be efficient. The dulling of incentives could result

---

[5] *Choice in Welfare*, Institute of Economic Affairs, London, July, 1963; discussed by Ralph Harris and Arthur Seldon, "Welfare and Choice," *The New Society*, July 25, 1963, pp. 14–16; and cited in James M. Buchanan, *op. cit.*, p. 193.

[6] *Ibid.*, pp. 241–266.

from both taxes and disbursements, which could make leisure or inefficiency less expensive to both the taxpayer and the recipient of welfare payments. As noted above, some transfers, by raising aspirations and the conviction that effort can bring rewards, may sharpen incentives, and they may have complicated income effects, but they will also tend to cause some substitution of leisure and convenience for work. (Similarly, generosity with one's children can produce desirable incentive effects but, if pressed too far or if handled ineptly, it can yield undesirable effects.) As a matter of fact, several possible losses of utility to be noted are simply the reverse of the possible gains previously noted. That is, in several instances, the effects are uncertain, and one actually anticipates a probability distribution of possible outcomes—with some probabilities of various amounts of gain and other probabilities of various amounts of loss of utility. On all these matters, of course, few persons would find it economical to think about the issues in a highly sophisticated fashion; instead they would make rough judgments or use crude rules of thumb.

(6) A possible disutility could arise from a belief that it is wrong from the standpoint of morality or the maintenance of self-respect for you or others to accept these transfers. A generation or so ago this was a powerful factor affecting utility. Numerous persons refused to accept benefits or to approve transfer programs. (7) Another minus that is the reverse of an item mentioned previously would be the possible loss of approval or support by your friends and associates—if they happen to dislike the transfer program. And, as mentioned above in the opposite case of the gain in utility, this consideration will be extremely important if you are a politician or public official. (8) As always, a reason for losing utility might be labeled "ideology"—an opposition to government expansion or to the transfer program because of your general beliefs, apart from the factors already mentioned. (9) Another possible loss would be any undesirable dynamic impacts—for example, impacts on the probabilities that the utility-maximization process will then lead to undesirable future legislation. For one action or piece of legislation affects the chances of success of other actions and thence the anticipated costs and rewards from actions. Thus, even if you approve of a particular transfer program as far as its immediate effects are concerned, you may disapprove of it because of anticipated repercussions on the shape of things to come. Or, even if you would disapprove of the consequences in a static sense, you may support the program because of its anticipated effects on future programs.

As noted previously, one such loss of utility could arise if you believed the appeasement or encouragement offered by a transfer program would make more probable a breakdown of law and order. For instance, a subsidy to the Ku Klux Klan, or to a group containing many subversives, or of such a nature that it would arouse widespread resentment could undermine the maintenance of order. Or you might be convinced that a transfer program would lead to a change in the decision-making rules—for example, that Federal urban redevelopment subsidies would undermine the authority of local governments, leading to increased centralization of authority. Some transfers might give more impetus to logrolling, leading to a heavier price to be paid to maintain the bargaining mechanism or to a revulsion against the bargaining process and a shift toward centralization of authority. As a consequence such transfers could lead to a reduction in adaptability and even in the likelihood of maintaining certain freedoms (see Chapter 7).

where does this process lead?

In the end each person's decision about his attitude toward a transfer program is somewhat similar to his decision about making a voluntary personal donation to a charity. There are usually numerous considerations involved, and the person asks himself, "Is the good or package of gains, as I see it, worth the costs as I perceive them?" The more rewarding or less expensive a program becomes to a voter, the greater the degree of his approval or the less the degree of his disapproval. The larger the number of voters who are affected in this way, the greater the degree of approval by organizations and producers of information. Information about the opinions of individuals and organization leaders spreads. Each legislator forms impressions about the consequences, in terms of support by colleagues and officials and voters, of his adopting alternative stands or voting behavior. The more rewarding or less expensive a proposal becomes to a legislator, the greater the degree of his approval or the less the degree of his disapproval. The larger the number of legislators affected in this way, the greater the chances of enactment. Thus the effects of a shift in the views of voters are somewhat similar to those of a shift in the tastes of consumers.

Most government-produced packages are handled on a yes-or-no basis, of course. Increments are considered, and the group can have more or less of each package, but different individuals cannot decide to have different amounts of the output—for example, to have only a small amount or none of the Medicare program if the bargaining mechanism leads to a decision to have a large Medicare program. If dissenters are willing to pay a very high price to try for the policy they prefer, they can demonstrate, break various laws, resort to violence, or try to start a civil war. Such things have often happened. Before deciding upon such actions, however, dissenters should make rather careful cost-gain calculations. Unless they have considerable strength, they stand to lose more than they would gain by risking a settlement by force. Doing that would be somewhat like my saying to Rocky Marciano, "Let's go out in the alley and find out who is right on this issue." To a considerable extent, therefore, utility maximization leads us to abide by (albeit to modify) decision-making rules. It is *usually* better for an individual to accept the results of the market in the private sphere than to turn to violence. (Of course, managers and union leaders and others try to get legislation enacted to gain shelter from competition and thus to alter the results.) With respect to government activities, it is *usually* better to accept the results of majority rule and existing institutions than to turn to violence, even when outcomes greatly displease particular groups, though such groups often deem it worthwhile to try for special favors or changes in the rules.

Where is all this likely to lead? The answer depends upon what goes into individuals' cost-gain "T-accounts" and on what policies become relatively expensive or inexpensive. To voters, the answer depends importantly on what weights they attach to several subtle, long-run, and uncertain repercussions on elements of their utility functions. In the case of policy producers the entries in the T-accounts depend greatly upon what kind of a bargaining mechanism is maintained. Policy producers and policy consumers will adapt their behavior according to these circumstances. Just as entrepreneurs in the private sector look for profitable opportunities and try to exploit them, so entrepreneurs in the public sector look for utility-gaining opportunities and try to exploit them. In general the process in democracies appears to result in decisions that are fairly responsive to the demands of large blocs of people. Yet it can also bring about incredible treatment of small uninfluential minorities. For example, during World War II, the bank accounts of many Japanese-Americans in the United States were confiscated; and in 1966, after years of dispute, U.S. courts disallowed the attempt by Congress to return these balances to those whose deposit receipts were not filed in the proper sixty-day period!

Over the past few decades, individuals' T-accounts have changed a good deal in the United States. Some of the plusses from transfer programs have increased, and some of the minuses have decreased. This has led to a rapid expansion of price-support programs (intended mainly as transfers); of Social Security, unemployment, veterans', and now Medicare benefits; and of grants-in-aid to state and local governments. Redistribution is also an important aim in many expanded activities that are not labeled transfer programs, such as housing subsidies, certain education programs, and minimum-wage legislation. Most of these transfers are relatively expensive to citizens of local governments acting alone (since people move in to take advantage of the benefits), so one would expect expansions to occur mostly at the Federal level. Even to officials of the Federal government, further expansions of Social Security and reimbursements of medical expenses may now appear to be costly, and one might expect the rate of expansion to slow down. Whenever other objectives, such as national defense, increase in importance (other things remaining the same), transfer programs look more costly to voters and therefore to officials, and one would expect a decline in their growth rate.

Reductions in transfers are rather difficult to bring about; the utility of a benefit expected with certainty is greater than that of a potential benefit anticipated with, say, 0.5 probability; and the loss if an existing benefit is eliminated therefore seems to exceed the loss if a potential benefit does not materialize. Because of this and other factors affecting their net utilities, beneficiaries often invest more effort in protecting an existing transfer program than in pressing for new ones (of equal magnitude).

The high costs of information (especially about the spill-in cost to each taxpayer from increased probabilities of future transfers to other groups) may produce a bias in favor of trades of transfer programs by different groups. Nations may end up with a bewildering and perhaps paralyzing network of transfer payments, going well beyond the arrangements in France, where it is sometimes said that "everyone has his deal."[7] Or they may move toward the outcome described in an early James Cagney movie: The strong take it away from the weak, and the smart take it away from the strong. Or individuals may become more concerned about long-run effects and shape the nature and scope of transfers so as to yield results that most persons would regard as more desirable. The model discussed in this chapter and in Chapter 2 is consistent with a broad spectrum of outcomes. To make better predictions, a better understanding of utility-maximization and group decision-making must be developed.

response of beneficiaries, administrators, and others

One aspect of transfer programs that each person should keep in mind in making his cost-gain calculations is that other persons involved in choosing, implementing, and reacting to such programs are also utility maximizers. That is, in assessing the effects of transfer payments, citizens should look *realistically* at the impacts on incentives and the behavior of administrators, recipients of the transfer payments, and others. None will be seeking solely to maximize his monetary wealth; but neither will any of them feel a burning, overriding desire to maximize GNP, promote economic efficiency, or achieve an equitable distribution of wealth.

Consider, for instance, transfers that are accomplished by reimbursing medical costs or providing hot lunches, freeways, water, housing, or anything else below cost. (All these activities involve transfers, though some do not officially

---

[7] Warren C. Baum, *The French Economy and the State*, Princeton University Press, Princeton, N.J., 1958, p. 353.

bear this label.) People are going to demand more than they would if they had to pay the cost. They will substitute these items for other things, put them to less important uses, utilize them less carefully, and demand more goods in which these subsidized items are ingredients. If larger quantities of the items sold below cost are not offered for sale, there will be shortages at the below-cost price; queues and congestion; rationing according to criteria (e.g., color or other personal characteristics) other than willingness to pay; opportunities for administrators to give special favors to some; incentives for mutually advantageous but inequitable deals; incentives to violate the spirit or the letter of the law; and, of course, pressures by some citizens and officials to make larger quantities available.

The fact that information is costly, in conjunction with individual utility maximization, is responsible for many of the consequences. To appraise effects of policies realistically, therefore, one must keep in mind how expensive information is. If information about people's characters, their means, their abilities, their health, their actions, and so on was available without cost—if each of us possessed an infallible crystal ball—administrators could ration these transfers to "deserving persons," make it costly for others to share in the transfer, render it too costly for undesired behavior to ensue, insure that subordinates acted in accordance with higher-level administrators' wishes, and thus produce precisely the desired effects. Voters might disagree about the definition of deserving persons, but they would be fully aware of what was going on and what they disagreed about. Majority coalitions (though not dissenters) could insure that legislators and top administrators behaved in accordance with their wishes in setting up transfer programs. The high cost of information, however, means that all this is a dream: transfer programs are in fact virtually certain to lead to means tests and other crude rationing devices, to abuses and inefficiences and inequities. Without careful planning of the constraints to be placed on beneficiaries and administrators, there can easily be too many constraints and paralyzed programs or too few constraints and a morass of abuses and inequities. In any event there are bound to be heavy costs of one sort or another (just as in the conduct of private charities there are bound to be either heavy administrative costs or abuses, again because of information costs). When voters buy transfer programs, they should recognize these shortcomings—just as, when they buy typewriters, they recognize that the machines will not be made of gold.

A realistic view of individuals' reactions often reveals hidden inequities in programs that are intended to promote equity. Each time Social Security coverage was expanded, persons in equal circumstances were often treated unequally. Individuals just short of age sixty-five who suddenly became eligible for coverage could contribute for only a short time and receive as much benefit as others in similar circumstances who had contributed for many years. Often women who are compelled to contribute do not work long enough to acquire eligibility at all. Such effects do not damn the Social Security system, but they should be recognized in designing and deciding about such transfer programs.

Much more striking are the perhaps hidden impacts of minimum-wage and equal-pay laws. These are not, strictly speaking, transfer programs, yet they are clearly intended to influence the distribution of wealth. Equal-pay laws are presumably intended to assure more equitable treatment of female employees, yet one of their effects is often to preclude the employment of women. If he must pay the same wage, the utility-maximizing employer usually prefers a man, because the higher probability of his staying with the firm, his greater flexibility, and his greater administrative potential make his value to the firm greater than that of a comparable female employee. (Needless to say, the employer must base his choice on clues and labels, such as "male" and "female," that convey probabilistic information, since to acquire full knowledge of each applicant would cost more than it would be worth.)

Minimum-wage programs are intended to help the poor, yet they do not work entirely in that direction. They make the less competent, poorly trained, inexperienced, or handicapped workers unemployable. This follows from the understandable adaptations of utility-maximizing employers to the laws. Again, these inequities do not damn the minimum-wage or equal-pay programs. They are simply disutilities (whose magnitudes depend on various elasticities of response) that should be taken into account realistically.

Underlying all this is the fundamental fact that the magnitude of people's reactions is uncertain. This basic truth, that the consequences of such transfer programs are uncertain, should be emphasized. Among other things it might prevent many dogmatic statements, ulcers, and unconstructive quarrels, but the main thing is that recognition of uncertainty is essential to choosing preferredness. Consider, for instance, government activities to break up ghettos and promote integration, which could be viewed, if one speaks loosely, as programs to redistribute opportunities or individual rights or the "stock of dignity." On the one hand, failure to take these steps may bring anything from inequity to catastrophe. On the other hand, taking these steps may have enormous favorable impacts, trivial favorable effects, or adverse consequences (by aggravating conflicts). Despite strong assertions, the consequences cannot be predicted with precision, particularly since a multitude of other variables will also be affecting events. It is the utility of these uncertain outcomes that should be weighed against the utility of the uncertain costs.

what should be done?

Should the U.S. government introduce more transfer programs or fewer of them or differently designed programs? As in the case of other decisions made when people live in groups, there are no demonstrably correct answers. One can only rank sets of policies according to his own preferences. Even for an individual, choosing is extremely difficult, for many of the costs and gains as he perceives them stem from subtle and uncertain, though crucial, effects. Thus all that analyses can do is to trace out some of the consequences of alternative programs and courses of action. To do this, analyses should look at human actions as resultants of utility maximization by individuals. And of course such studies should look at the utility-maximization process in the context of particular institutional arrangements. As they perceive this process and these various consequences more clearly, individuals can make *their* choices in the light of better information, though there will never be a set of transfers that is correct from some mystical "group viewpoint."

five

Another major aim of government spending is to influence resource allocation among uses. As mentioned in the previous chapter, it is useful to discuss these broad aims or "products" of government separately, even though any program is bound to affect numerous aims simultaneously. The ways in which government influences resource allocation include subsidies (and taxes), exhortation of industrial or union leaders by public officials, bargaining or persuasion, regulation, prohibition, procurement, extension of credit, and government production. All these devices can affect, though to varying degrees, the costs or rewards from putting resources to particular uses and thus influence resource allocation. Specific programs will not be examined in detail; rather, the chapter will discuss some of the important factors bearing on these public spending choices.

Why should government choose to influence resource allocation? In general terms, the reason is that, with individual utility maximization, majority coalitions turn out to be willing to buy these activities, and politician-entrepreneurs are therefore willing to produce them. But why do certain resource-reallocation programs become relatively salable? The underlying reason is interdependency—the fact that one man's action or lack of action affects other persons. If A's behavior did not impinge *in any way* on B, neither A nor B would ask for governmental intervention. In real life B is involved, though; there are always possibilities of taking something from A, buying something from him, cooperating with him in securing some joint objective, or reducing damages caused by him.

Many interdependencies result in contracts, or tacitly understood agreements, that make A willing to produce beneficial things for B, and C willing to let A use (i.e., "damage") his time, energy, comfort, or machinery. This eliminates much potential concern (though some persons may still press for transfer programs). Often many interdependencies remain, however, that are not recognized, compensated for, and voluntarily accepted. These are the externalities or spillovers, and their existence often leads to the willingness of voters and officials to approve measures encouraging, discouraging, or producing certain outputs. Before utility maximization is discussed in this connection, it is important to understand the nature of externalities and of the set of outputs called "public goods."

externalities[1]

Externalities are those effects of production or consumption processes that are not exerted through markets, i.e., that are not taken into account through voluntary exchange.[2] They are really just a particular set of interdependencies. As mentioned in Chapters 2 and 3, many interdependencies are "internalized" through voluntary exchange and might be called "internalities." For example, if one uses an acre of land in a production process but obtains it through voluntary trade, that is, by leasing it, the cost is an "internality." If one can and does use an acre of land by letting salt water seep underneath it without buying the consent of the owner, this cost is an externality. If a person's consumption of alcohol uses up the quietness of his neighbor's atmosphere, but he leases this resource from the neighbor, it is an internal cost—merely the

---

[1] There is an extensive literature on externalities. The following articles have been especially helpful to me: James M. Buchanan and Wm. Craig Stubblebine, "Externality," *Economica*, November, 1962, pp. 371–384; Ronald H. Coase, "The Problem of Social Cost," *Journal of Law and Economics*, October, 1960, pp. 1–44; and Harold Demsetz, "The Exchange and Enforcement of Property Rights," *Journal of Law and Economics*, October, 1964, pp. 11–26.

At numerous places in the next two sections I am particularly indebted to Demsetz.

[2] Some economists elect to define externalities as "any effects on other persons," but I think the term is more valuable as a label for the subset than as a synonym for interdependencies.

hiring of another input. If the noise goes on without the neighbor's consent, its cost is an externality.

On the benefit side, if a man produces apples and sells them to a customer at prices satisfactory to both parties, this benefit to the consumer is internalized and taken into account by the producer. If for some reason he cannot arrange to charge for his apple output, then the benefit to those who take the apples is an externality. Since no one, or at least no private firm, is likely to produce outputs completely without compensation, external benefits usually appear to be by-products of the production of some output that is marketed. But to label them by-products or minor (or major) products serves no useful purpose; they are simply certain outputs or effects—certain interdependencies— that are not approved by means of a voluntary exchange.

One reason external effects exist is that the costs of defining, exchanging, and policing rights to benefits, or rights not to be afflicted with damages, sometimes exceed the gains to private groups from "internalizing" these effects.[3] Policing or enforcing *any* right is costly. If one produces apples, there is expense in protecting one's right to them while they are on the trees, in the warehouse, or in the stores. When consumers buy apples, there is a cost to them of guarding the apples until consumed. If a firm uses an input such as sulfuric acid, there is expense involved in protecting the rights of others to adjacent assets when the firm uses the acid or pours off the waste. But sometimes the cost of defining and enforcing a right is extremely high. For example, it turns out to be particularly expensive to define, enforce, and exchange rights to airspace into which no one can with impunity pour air pollutants or extra decibels of sound. It would be very costly for homeowners to arrange to be compensated for noise by contracting with the numerous and transient operators of power lawnmowers or municipal trash-collection trucks. (Alternatively, it would be extremely expensive for the noisemakers to contract with homeowners to create less noise for a fee.) As another example, Sid Caesar is said to have the kinescopes of 482 television programs from his "Show of Shows." Benefit to viewers from reruns would exceed the cost of presenting them. But this benefit is not produced. The reason, it is alleged, is that the original contracts made no mention of reruns, and it would now be necessary to renegotiate with so many persons that the expense would be prohibitive. In numerous instances, then, the costs of negotiating agreements would exceed the gains to the parties concerned. In such situations life is not as beautiful as it might be in some ideal world, but seemingly no way can be devised to improve it by voluntary agreement.

---

[3] Demsetz has greatly clarified the implications of "policing" and contracting or "transaction" costs (Demsetz, *op. cit.*).

It is conceivable, of course, that everyone is being unperceptive and that ingenuity *can* currently find a way to reduce these costs and internalize the external effects. But suppose this is not so. One might then consider various government actions. In many instances, a majority might agree that these actions too would cost more than they would be worth. Suppose the least expensive way to eliminate sound intrusion was to ban automobiles, airplanes, power saws, and power lawnmowers. Not many persons would really vote for that. Again one might have to conclude that life is imperfect but that no action which would improve it (for a majority of voters) can be perceived. (And one should not forget that unimprovable imperfection is the same thing as perfection.)

In another category of cases it may appear to an individual or to whatever group is in control that prohibition, public regulation, or government production *would* gain more than it would cost. As an illustration, while I would not vote for prohibition of noise-making machinery, I would vote for quite stringent restrictions on the production of noise. On a day when I am at home, the piecemeal removal of a tree with a power saw, even a block away, inflicts more damage on me than would the smashing of my front windows. In another set of cases, it may not be economical now to do anything about an externality— yet with changes in tastes, technology, and resources, it may later become economical to internalize it by voluntary trade or to have government intervention. The optimal sizes of firms and the contractual arrangements in shopping centers have changed over time as certain external benefits have become important enough to be worth internalizing and capturing. In the past, air pollution and noise may usually have been trivial external costs, yet because of urbanization and technological change they may now warrant new contractual arrangements or increased government intervention. Thus there are several subsets of external effects, and it is probably helpful to keep these subsets in mind.

One externality, the involuntary emission or deliberate theft of information, is growing in significance because of the increasing value of information and the changing technology of acquiring it. With economic growth and rapid change, information about employment opportunities, the prospects for new ventures, the skills and capabilities of individuals, the actions and plans of rival firms (not to mention the actions and plans of rival nations), the existence and profitability of new processes, the performance characteristics of products, etc., has become increasingly valuable. (In a static situation, information would have less value.) But information, and misinformation, flow almost like light waves or bacteria through the air, and only a fraction of the interdependencies stemming from information flows is internalized by voluntary agreement. Often government actions—the patent system and revisions of it, subsidies to education, government crop reports and employment exchanges, legislation to discourage wiretapping—have been deemed appropriate to cope with information flows. But rights are still unclear, and other actions regarding these externalities may be worth their cost. Moreover, a great deal of technological change in the production of information is occurring. The use of satellites for weather prediction, of miniature microphones and cameras, and of easy ways to tap phones or overhear conversations a block away are examples of changes that may lead to additional, or more serious, external effects. Indeed it has apparently become economical for special firms to exist whose task is to "debug" corporations' conference rooms prior to meetings of the boards of directors—that is, to reduce the externality of involuntary information leakage.

To cope with potential externalities in the face of the high costs of making explicit agreements, people through the centuries have evolved many tacit agreements or rules of etiquette.[4] Quite early in the development of civilized man it must have become apparent that extreme rudeness, bickering, taking advantage of others as far as explicit contracts would allow, complete indifference to the misfortune or infirmity of others, etc., involved external costs, retaliation, and ultimately high costs for everyone—costs that could probably be reduced. Even without conscious thought about the matter, it must also have been obvious that explicit, detailed agreements among individuals enforceable in some court system, or detailed laws about etiquette enforceable through courts, would be extremely expensive. The economical arrangements that evolved consisted of general rules enforceable through social pressure. In ordinary circumstances, annoying neighbors, insulting colleagues, berating secretaries, or cursing old ladies soon make other people similarly indifferent to their oppressors' comfort, not necessarily out of revenge but simply because it does not pay the sufferers to be concerned about the rude persons' feelings. As a consequence, there would be unnecessarily high costs all around. Most of us get the message and stay within the range of expected behavior, at least most of the time. Voluntary agreements to internalize what would otherwise be externalities are at times, therefore, rather imprecise tacit agreements that are enforced only by social pressures.

public goods[5]

So much for externalities, at least for the moment. What do they have to do with "public goods"? The latter are goods and services which are particularly likely to cause externalities. Their distinctive feature is that they can be con-

---

[4] Armen A. Alchian called the basic idea to my attention.

[5] Basic references on this topic include: Paul A. Samuelson, "The Pure Theory of Public Expenditure," *Review of Economics and Statistics*, November, 1954, pp. 387–

sumed by more than one person at the same time at no extra expense; and it actually costs something to exclude potential consumers. If one man eats an apple or makes use of an electrician's time, he automatically prevents anyone else from consuming that same item. But consider such outputs as television and radio programs, band concerts, and football games. The lowest-cost way of producing these items is such that one person can enjoy them without decreasing another person's enjoyment of them—at least up to a certain number of viewers or listeners. If it were possible (without incurring extra costs to exclude others) to produce band concerts so that they were audible to only one person, or baseball games that were visible to only one person, then anyone who listened or watched would prevent someone else from doing so. If TV transmission could be expanded point by point as cheaply as area by area, it could be produced, like shoes or apples, in units that could without extra cost be consumed by one person at a time. In reality, though, additional persons up to a point can listen to a band concert, hear a radio program, or watch a rodeo without preventing anyone else from doing so; it would cost extra to make these goods available to one person at a time. The feature that makes these goods different is that certain light, sound, scent, health, domestic-security and national-security "emissions" cover an area rather than a spot the size of a human body.

Strictly speaking, of course, persons farther from the bandstand, playing field, or transmission facilities get "poorer reception," and, therefore, one man's consumption may *partially* prevent another man from consuming. Indeed, as serious congestion arises, one man's consumption will almost totally prevent someone else from using the service, and beyond that point the public-good characteristics of the item disappear. But at least two persons can watch a rodeo as easily as one. Incidentally, television and radio may appear to be different from the other cases, because within a given area the point at which serious congestion would arise is rather remote. The population of television and radio receivers would have to be very dense indeed to impair anyone else's use of these electronic emissions. Yet there is no difference in principle. Congestion could occur eventually, just as it does when people are crowded into less desirable seats at a baseball game.

As noted before, it costs something to enforce one man's rights to any good, such as an apple, by preventing theft or damage by others. But one can charge

---

390, and "Aspects of Public Expenditure Theories," *Review of Economics and Statistics,* November, 1958, pp. 332–338; Richard A. Musgrave, *The Theory of Public Finance,* McGraw-Hill Book Company, New York, 1959, especially pp. 9, 10, and 73–86. The uncertainty about what public-good policies are Pareto-optimal, while recognized by others, has been emphasized by Jora R. Minasian, "Television Pricing and the Theory of Public Goods," *Journal of Law and Economics,* October, 1964, pp. 71–80.

a "price of admission," and there is no problem of excluding others from *simultaneous* consumption. For public goods, such as products that involve sound- or light-wave emission, however, there is an additional cost if nonpayers are to be excluded so that a price of admission can be charged. To exclude potential viewers of an athletic event, one has to build a stadium or wall. Excluding persons from the benefits of noise abatement (a public good since one man's consumption of it does not reduce another person's use of it) is difficult even to visualize.

To repeat, the distinctive feature of public goods (and public "bads") is the high cost of confining the benefits (or damages) to selected persons and of charging admission (or buying permission to damage). Usually it is feasible to exclude nonpayers—for example, by erecting enclosures, creating barriers to light or sound waves, devising scramblers for radio and television emissions, expelling individuals or regions from a political jurisdiction—but the exclusion costs something, and sometimes the costs would be extremely high.

Some goods, it might be noted, are public with respect to a subset of the population yet not public goods with respect to the whole population. For example, individuals within a designated river valley cannot be excluded from a flood-control program. Thus a price of admission can be charged to each subset, even though a price of admission to individuals within each subset is presumably impossible. This would be true regarding many local services.

Why do public goods often yield externalities? Because this cost of excluding potential beneficiaries and charging admission—or, for public bads, the extra costs of preventing damage to those unwilling to suffer it for agreed-upon compensations—means that it will often be uneconomic to do so. In such instances, if the good is produced, there will be external effects.

Public goods are not the only ones that result in externalities, because private goods may be produced under conditions which make it uneconomical to dispose of those goods by voluntary exchange. For example, fish are not public goods; if one man eats a fish, no one else can consume it. Yet a farmer may have a pond in which fish having some value grow, and it may not be economical to enforce the rights to these fish and market them. Nor do public bads account for all external costs. Letting waste acid flow onto one neighbor's acreage does not simultaneously damage other lands. Yet it may yield an externality—a cost about which there is no voluntary agreement.[6] There is another reason that public goods are not identical with items that yield externalities. In addition to the fact that other goods sometimes result in externalities, some public goods do *not* result in externalities. When it is economical to erect

---

[6] Or consider throwaway papers or handbills left on lawns: why don't the "throwers" have to buy the consent of householders? Because of contracting costs; no public-good characteristic, or cost of exclusion, is involved.

barriers and charge admission, as in the case of commercial entertainment, there *may* be no external effects—for example, no costs or benefits that side payments would elicit—if the fee happens to equal marginal congestion costs. Nonetheless, while not accounting for all externalities and not always producing externalities, public goods and bads do yield many of them, for it is frequently uneconomical to internalize the effects.

Like externalities, public goods can be divided into sets or categories, and it is probably useful to keep these categories in mind. First of all, there are two general types: (1) those that end up in the private sector because it is economical to exclude potential users and charge admission, and (2) those that are not produced voluntarily by private entrepreneurs because exclusion and negotiation prove to be too costly. Examples of the first category include motion pictures and plays, many athletic events and concerts, some lectures and speeches, circuses, and indeed most forms of entertainment for profit. Public goods in the second category may be left unproduced, produced in the private sector as a tie-in sale with advertising (as in the case of commercial television), produced in the private sector with the aid of government subsidy or perhaps with government constraints, or produced by the public sector. Examples are provided by smog abatement and noise abatement. Some of these outputs prove to be profitable in the private sector, as individuals contract with each other to reduce noise or air pollution, or, more often, unilaterally install air conditioning or thicker walls to shield themselves from noise or air pollution. But most abatement of smog and noise is not produced by the private sector voluntarily. Some is produced in that sector as a result of government subsidy or taxes or regulatory constraints. Some is produced by government, which refrains from repairing streets at night in residential areas or adopts processes or measures that reduce the noise level or the injection of pollutants. Much abatement of smog and noise is simply left unproduced, because so far it is deemed uneconomical to produce it.

Secondly, there are other subsets or categories into which it may be useful to sort public goods: (1) pure public goods, (2) mixed public goods, and (3) part of output a public good. These distinctions have been hinted at earlier, but the distinctions have not been brought out clearly.

A pure public good is one that (1) potential consumers cannot be excluded from without extra costs and (2) *given the production of the good,* can be consumed by an additional person at zero marginal cost. The output of the strategic deterrent force is perhaps the best example. Excluding anyone who did not "buy a ticket" would be extremely expensive. It would involve something like deportation (expensive because it would imply drastic changes in values and political processes, which might in turn be rather costly to everyone) or announcing to foreign countries that the defense department was not protecting the list of persons who were unwilling to buy the deterrent program (expensive because allowing nations to attack those individuals would also endanger the others). In fact the costs of exclusion would be so high that no one believes it would make sense to charge admission. Moreover, the marginal cost of allowing another person to consume the benefits of existing deterrence is zero. That is, use of this commodity by one more resident of the United States does not deprive anyone else of its benefits or entail any other sort of cost—*given the existence of the deterrent force*. Note, however, that the cost in the sense of alternative deterrent programs sacrificed (or other foregone uses of the resources) is not zero, for *continued* production is *not* given. One can imagine a force consisting of billions of rabbits' feet and tons of wolfsbane. Some people might believe this would deter thermonuclear attack, but others might prefer a different use of the resources.

Radio and television are other examples of pure public goods. It costs something extra for a descrambling system to exclude certain potential users, and—given a program that is already on the air—the marginal cost of allowing another person to tune in is zero. Again it should be remembered, however, that putting one program on the air entails the sacrifice of alternative programs that might have been broadcast. In the United States this public good is largely in the private sector because of the tie-in sale with advertising, though pay-TV may yet prove to be economical. That is, admission charges might be able to cover all costs including the costs of excluding potential viewers who do not pay the price of admission. (If the choice is ever left to the market, the programs that survive will probably be somewhat like the magazines that survive—a mixture of programs paid for partly by viewers but containing moderate amounts of advertising, a few programs paid for exclusively by viewers, and some "throwaway" programs paid for exclusively by advertisers.)

The term "mixed public good" is sometimes used to mean a good that (1) consumers cannot be costlessly excluded from, and (2) given the production of the item, can be enjoyed by an additional consumer at a marginal cost that is positive but is below average cost. The reason that the marginal cost of having another user is positive is that congestion begins to occur so that packing in another viewer or listener does reduce the comfort and utility of other consumers. Consider a sandlot baseball game or a band concert. Even with the production of the item given, adding to the audience beyond some point does interfere with the enjoyment of the others, i.e., does entail some cost, though it need bear no particular relationship to average cost. Again note that continued production is not really given, and alternative concerts, games, or myriad other uses of these resources *are* being sacrificed. To take an extreme case: If the band simply played an endless version of "Three Blind Mice," it is not true that nothing would be sacrificed by people in the aggregate or by the marginal listener.

Sometimes the term "mixed public good" is used in another sense—namely, to mean an instance in which *part* of the output of a production process is a public good. Consider smallpox immunization. Part of the output, the benefit to the person being vaccinated, is not a public good at all. His use of the vaccine automatically prevents anyone else from consuming the vaccine and being immunized. Another part of the output, the benefit to others because of the lower probability of encountering smallpox germs, is a public good. It can be enjoyed by millions as well as by one. My use of this lower probability does not reduce the value of it to anyone else, and it would cost a great deal to exclude nonpayers from enjoying this benefit so that admission could be charged to it. Education is like an immunization program in these respects. If one person uses a book or other educational service, he prevents someone else from doing so. At the same time, there are benefits to nonusers (particularly from elementary schooling) that float through the air, so to speak. It would be expensive to set up barriers to exclude those who refused to buy a ticket from enjoying the indirect benefits of having a literate, reasonably articulate population holding many values and beliefs in common; and the use of these benefits by one person does not reduce anyone else's consumption of them.

Judicial and law-enforcement systems are also mixed public goods in this sense (or, if they are vicious arrangements, mixed public bads). Part of the output, the settlement of particular claims, is a nonpublic good, and consumption by one precludes someone else from consuming the same item, that is, the particular inquiry and decision. Much of the output, however, is simply an altered environment that yields pervasive benefits. It would be quite costly to exclude nonpayers from enjoying these benefits so that admission could be charged. And, given its production, the use of this environment by one individual does not detract from another individual's ability to consume it.

pricing of public goods if pareto optimality is sought

So much for the nature of public goods. What implications do they have for public spending policies? In general terms the answer is that goods having these characteristics often call for at least the consideration of government intervention. Whenever it is decided to intervene, this decision affects how much the government spends and the way it is spent. What should governments do? Let us inquire into the production and pricing of public goods, making the oversimplified assumption that Pareto optimality is the agreed-upon goal.

It is generally argued that the achievement of full economic efficiency calls for the marginal-cost pricing of all goods—that is, pricing that reflects the value of the marginal alternatives foregone. This principal is a correct one, but just what marginal cost amounts to is sometimes unclear. It is unclear in connection with public goods. As mentioned earlier, the marginal cost of allowing another person to enjoy a public good is zero, *once the good has been produced*. But continued production is not preordained, and the cost of charging a zero price is not zero, for one then sacrifices information about individuals' preferences regarding subsequent investment and production decisions. If Pareto optimality is the criterion, this information has value, and sacrificing it is a cost. Moreover it is a marginal cost, because the greater the output and the more consumers served without determining individual preferences, the greater the sacrifice of valuable information. But there is no separate market for this information, and one does not know how great this sacrifice or cost is.

To make this point clearer, consider an illustration mentioned before. The municipal band could play "Three Blind Mice" over and over again. If a price of admission were not charged, there would be no marketing process to reveal whether or not people preferred some other use of the resources.[7] Producing this good and charging a zero price would ignore this information cost and neglect options. The political process would not actually permit the gross neglect of alternatives that this Three Blind Mice example reflects. But neither should the careless interpretation of rules purporting to point the way to economic efficiency.

One can try in other ways to obtain the information sacrificed, but only by incurring costs. Perhaps it should be noted that this is not a trivial consideration. Markets do a fantastic job of generating data regarding prospective costs and gains.[8] And attempting to prepare cost-benefit analyses of alternative government actions makes one realize how difficult it is to provide such knowledge without markets.[9] Indeed to provide information about marginal evaluations *that is comparable in quality* to the knowledge generated by markets is often infinitely expensive, i.e., impossible.

Incidentally, durability does not alter the general argument. In principle, it

[7] Musgrave, *op. cit.*, p. 10.

The basic point is an old one—that when an enterprise is operated at a deficit made up by government, by other receipts in a "basin account," or by users of other commodities, we lose guidance regarding the design of the output and the selection of future investment. See Ronald H. Coase, "The Marginal Cost Controversy," *Economica*, August, 1946, pp. 169–182.

[8] Harold Demsetz, "Some Aspects of Property Rights," *Journal of Law and Economics* (forthcoming).

[9] Roland N. McKean, "The Use of Shadow Prices in Evaluating Federal Expenditure Programs," The Brookings Institution, Second Conference on Government Expenditures, September, 1966.

is immaterial whether the good will last five minutes or fifty years. Guidance regarding the subsequent expenditure decisions is valuable, whether they are to be made next day (scheduling the next day's radio or television program) or several years later (maintaining or expanding a bridge). For long-lived and almost unique assets like a particular bridge, however, the information about consumers' bids has a relatively low value *if* it will be many years before any maintenance or expansion decision is to be made. In connection with assets about which choices will be made sooner, such as trucks, the information has greater value. In connection with assets that are not unique, such as most buildings, the information is valuable for continuous decisions about the replacement, maintenance, or creation of related assets. Thus *in the early life* of long-lasting resources for which close substitutes are not frequently produced, the information foregone by charging a zero price may not deserve any weight as a cost.

In any event, marginal costs of providing public goods are hard to discern. Pareto would not require one to charge a zero price, but it is not clear just what the pricing arrangement should be. Discriminatory or multipart pricing[10]—an initial lump payment plus subsequent payments equal to marginal cost in the conventional sense—would help in some instances where it is economical to exclude potential users and charge admission, though even there the appropriate policy is debatable. But in cases such as national defense where it is too expensive to exclude users and charge admission, the option of determining consumers' evaluations is simply not open, full marginal costs are indeterminate, and the rules for Pareto optimality provide no *operational* assistance. Personal judgments are inevitable even if people agree upon Pareto optimality as a goal.

All this adds up to one discouraging point. Even for achieving economic efficiency there are no clear-cut guidelines regarding the pricing and production of public goods. If it is profitable to exclude nonpayers and charge admission, it is better to have some of the good than to have none, though the possibility that government intervention could effect a further improvement cannot be ruled out. If it is not profitable for private ventures to exclude potential consumers unless they pay, one is left with still less guidance toward economic efficiency. To complicate matters further, government activity usually yields a mixture of public goods and public bads. Government outlays for health, education, recreation, highways, public housing, pollution abatement, urban renewal, and integration have public-good characteristics, that is, certain pervasive benefits which are not denied to some when they are bestowed on others and from which one cannot costlessly exclude potential users so as to charge admission. On the other hand, increases in government activity may produce other environmental effects that are public bads (or effects that reduce other public goods). For

---

[10] Coase, "The Marginal Cost Controversy."

example, changes in the environment that reduce adaptability or the probability of preserving and furthering individual rights (see Chapter 7) would be such public bads. Since several personal judgments are involved, one man can legitimately differ from another about what is Pareto-optimal.

utility maximization and resource-reallocation proposals

Needless to say, however, Pareto optimality is not the agreed-upon aim in choosing government activities. The goal of government officials is utility maximization, with individual costs and rewards shaped by their preference functions, by institutional arrangements, and by the bargaining process. The goal of voters and citizens, too, is utility maximization, with individual costs and rewards shaped by their preference functions, by institutional arrangements, and by myriad relationships with other persons. Insights about the way this works will be facilitated by a look at some of the elements of utility functions that are affected by resource-reallocation policies.

possible gains in utility to the individual

What are some of the favorable considerations that you might have in mind if you pondered a proposed irrigation project, public health program, educational subsidy, or urban-planning activity?

(1) A direct contribution to your wealth might be in the picture. The proposal might appear likely to expand the demand for your skills, increase the value of your land or other assets, or widen the range of your opportunities. Interesting differences in the size and impact of this item occur with differences in institutional arrangements and circumstances. For instance, as Buchanan has pointed out, if the stream of benefits is capitalized into an immediate increment in present value, the impact may be greater than it is if the stream of benefits cannot be capitalized into the value of some marketable asset.[11] Thus free water for irrigation may sharply increase the value of one's land, while free medical service or defense is not converted into a higher present value of one's land or marketable assets. (The counterpart of this phenomenon on the disutility side is that a rise in the property tax may be felt differently from a rise in the income tax.)

(2) You might expect to consume the public good or the subsidized good that would be produced. If housing, milk, or education were to be subsidized,

---

[11] James M. Buchanan, *Public Finance in Democratic Process: Fiscal Institutions and Individual Choice*, The University of North Carolina Press, Chapel Hill, N.C., 1967, pp. 66–70.

you would expect a larger gain, the higher your rate of use of these items. You could count on a large increment in utility from a government broadcasting station if you thought the programs would be to your liking. To some extent you would benefit from almost any good or service produced.

(3) You might anticipate receiving spillover benefits from extra consumption of the goods by other persons. If other members of the community are vaccinated or if their health is improved, you encounter fewer germs and other health hazards. (4) You might also foresee an indirect addition to your wealth if you believed the resource shifts would make the economy more efficient. You would have a stake in improved efficiency because increases in marginal productivities trickle down and around, as people adapt, and affect almost everyone. (5) You could attach value to increased efficiency for the sake of others, of your children, or of posterity in general. For example, when families have children and increase the population, they inflict costs on other persons without purchasing those persons' consent. Government policies to reduce this externality are apparently valued by many persons because they believe a small population would make their children or posterity better off. (6) You would presumably attach some positive utility to the receipt of benefits by other persons, because of the effects on the equity of wealth distribution or because of a feeling of obligation to the group that would be benefited or because of the pleasure of seeing anyone made a little better off. (This is the utility to you of the transfer aspects of the proposed program.) (7) You might also believe that these benefits to others—say in a distressed area—would yield a more stable society and better protect individual rights for you, your children, or for virtually everyone.

(8) You might gain utility from seeing certain kinds of consumption (such as liquor) discouraged or other kinds of consumption encouraged. You might believe that more religious training, reading, listening to classical music, watching good plays, or indoctrination with common beliefs and values would result in a better culture in some sense or a more stable society. This is sometimes a powerful motivation and properly so. Without *some* quantity of indoctrination, ritual, and cultivated consensus, it is doubtful if any organization—the Boy Scouts, a church, or a nation—could survive competition with rival organizations or attractions. (This source of utility might be extremely important to everyone if the effects of different kinds of reading, music, education, or indoctrination could be predicted with greater confidence.) (9) You might wish to have government provide goods because of your ideology or because you desire more control by government—such government activities might increase government officials' leverage. (You might feel this way especially if you were not in the groups likely to be controlled.) (10) You might look upon economic growth as a public good and place a high value on resource reallocations that

you believed would accelerate growth. (11) As always, a rich source of utility to almost everyone is obtaining the approval and avoiding the disapproval of friends, associates, superiors, and so on. If your constituents, employers, colleagues, or friends are enthusiastic about a resource-reallocation proposal, you will find at least a few "utils" associated with taking the same stand as your friends do.

where does utility maximization lead?

Possible losses to an individual from a proposal would include some of those described in Chapter 4 and the opposites of certain gains just described. It will be assumed that the sample of disutilities that people might consider is by this time sufficiently familiar. The next step is to ask, "In the light of these various considerations, what choices have been, or are likely to become, relatively expensive and what ones relatively inexpensive?"

Only a few elementary points will be suggested here. Utility maximization with institutions that require a good deal of bargaining does make public spending choices somewhat responsive to the preferences of large blocs of people. As world tensions unfolded during the past decades, it began to look increasingly expensive to voters (and thence to officials) to neglect national defense or, to look at the other side of the coin, increasingly rewarding to purchase more of this public good. The possible costs of neglecting space exploration were also impressive, though obviously there has been much disagreement about the proper scale of this program. With national growth and urbanization, utility maximizers feared not to give more attention to highway networks, pollution control, and urban difficulties. Some public goods appear to be growing in significance as capital and populations grow and as technology changes. One would expect this growth to induce more voters to call for government action and to demand ("buy") more resource-reallocation programs, particularly since information costs and decision costs often render opposition comparatively weak. Some of these "goods"—such as space exploration, defense, certain recreational facilities, and regional pollution abatement—appear to be relatively expensive or relatively unrewarding for local governments to buy, and one would expect them to buy relatively little of these items except by bargaining with other lower-level governments or with the central government.

As before, it is important, in taking one's position about spending proposals, to be realistic about the reactions of managers, householders, administrators, and laborers. In connection with urban-development proposals, it often seems that the probable reactions of people directly affected, or uncertainties about those reactions, are being neglected. Is the desired behavior being made *significantly* less expensive or rewarding? Subsidized housing, for example, is supposed to cause former slum dwellers to live in better accommodations and thence produce indirect benefits for much of the community. It can cause people to choose better housing if it (1) increases the wealth of the occupants or (2) makes *better* housing less expensive to them than before. Most subsidies increase the wealth of the occupants only slightly and do not make the *maintenance of better* housing much less expensive or more rewarding than before. One should not expect dramatic results if these shifts in costs or rewards are actually tiny from the standpoint of individual utility-maximizing occupants and residents.

Little is known about these matters—about how government measures affect the costs and rewards to individuals of alternative responses by them, or about the elasticities of response to given changes in cost-reward structures. Not much is known about the way the bargaining mechanism transforms the decisions of citizens into costs and rewards felt by officials and politicians. And little is known about the elasticities of response by government personnel and, therefore, about what actions they are likely to take. It is important to understand these things more fully, but it will require much hypothesis formulation and testing. As more is learned, citizens can make better choices from their individual standpoints. Although there is no set of public spending choices that is ultimately "*right*," or correct for *all*, perhaps people's wishes will be sufficiently similar to prompt government activities that seem comparatively desirable to most persons.

six

GOVERNMENT SPENDING AND FLUCTUATIONS

Another important impact of government expenditures is their contribution to the stabilization (or destabilization) of aggregate spending and the resultant consequences. Like an action affecting wealth distribution or resource allocation, a decision influencing stability also affects numerous additional elements in the utility functions of congressmen, officials, and voters. These individuals will determine their positions regarding particular proposals in the light of all the proposals' perceived effects on their utility. In this chapter, however, attention will be focused mainly on the one subset of effects—the possible impacts of spending choices on stability (and, through stability, on growth). Again decisions by the individual participants in the process will be stressed as the key to predicting government choices and perceiving subsequent choices and impacts.

First, background argument is presented about changes in aggregate spending as the cause of deflation and inflation, about the role of information and adjustment costs in producing unemployment, and about the causes of changes in aggregate spending. Then the effects of alternative spending policies on fluctuations are examined. Finally, after looking at some side effects of different types of national debt, and looking at some tools that may make better policies less expensive, the chapter briefly reexamines the question: Can there be such a thing as a "correct" policy?

cause of inflation and deflation

Total annual expenditures on final outputs comprise consumption plus investment plus government purchases. There are other ways in which one could break down total spending, but this is a common, and is generally believed to be a useful, way of "slicing" the total. This amount per year is determined by the spending decisions of millions of utility maximizers in households, business firms, and governmental jurisdictions. A later section will explore the events that can make increments or decrements in spending relatively rewarding to individuals. Our concern at the moment is simply with the connection between the rate of aggregate spending and inflation or deflation.

Aggregate annual expenditures equal prices of goods times quantities sold or, loosely speaking, output. As suggested above, it is usually convenient to talk about final output only—that is, to neglect intermediate transactions prior to consumption, investment, or government purchases. When total outlays are enough to buy the year's output of final goods and services at the existing price level, there is economic stability, that is, no general deflation or inflation.

If the rate of aggregate spending increases, either prices or output have to increase. If output cannot or does not increase, it is the price level that rises. That is what most people mean by inflation. If the rate of aggregate spending decreases, either output or prices or both must decline. Because of information and adjustment costs, many utility-maximizing owners of resources, including both employers and employees, will find no course of action better than being at least partly unemployed. As a consequence, the process of deflation that occurs when total spending falls always brings some decline of employment and output as well as a fall in the general price level. An understanding of this process is so important that it will be examined at considerable length. After all, a serious depression not only would sacrifice much material well-being but could affect the probabilities of having drastic changes in legislation, shifts in institutions and power structures, social upheavals, even wars among nations.

the role of information and adjustment costs[1]

Even without fluctuations of aggregate demand, information and adjustment costs produce unemployed resources. Millions of car owners leave their auto-

---

[1] The arguments here are taken from Armen A. Alchian's unpublished manuscript on the basic causes of unemployment.

mobiles idly parked several hours a day and most of each night. Thousands of items in the home—tables, chairs, desks, pictures on the wall, lamps, beds, utensils, and hi-fi sets—lie idle much of the time. The reason: it is less expensive to have this idle capacity than it would be to sell or rent the items to others when they are not in use and buy them back when wanted. To do the latter would be very expensive because of information and adjustment costs. It would be costly to calculate just when one would like to use the car or listen to the hi-fi set or look at the painting on the wall; and it would be costly to accept the consequences of bad calculations. It would be very costly to acquire information about who would be willing to rent or buy these items when not in use, to find out how much they would pay, to draw up contracts, and to move the resources back and forth—in short, it would be expensive to set up markets for these unused services. Except in unusual circumstances (sometimes, of course, people do rent their homes, cars, and other items)[2] it is less expensive, in producing a given level of utility, simply to provide unused capacity.

The same thing is as true for ordinary producers as it is for households viewed as producers. Business firms often find it economical to have unused capacity in desks, telephones, equipment, and buildings (especially at night and on weekends). Human beings, unskilled and skilled alike, have unused capacity too because of information and adjustment costs. It costs too much to find out just what demands will be made on one's time, just who would bid how much for one's idle moments; it costs too much to flit from one task to another one, perhaps several miles away. It is more economical for individuals to spend part of their time just waiting. (In the Army, where it is still more difficult to capture gains from various uses of one's time, it is economical to spend a larger amount of time just waiting). It is often efficient to have secretaries or assistants even if they must be kept idle part of the time; and one executive must sometimes wait for another executive.

When greater adjustments become appropriate and demands for a resource become more uncertain, periods of idleness may increase, for owners of the resources may find, over still longer periods, no employment that is preferable to waiting and acquiring information. Suppose a man has just graduated from college or a building has just been constructed. Or suppose a man has just lost his job or a building has just become vacant. It would be a misuse of resources if the man or the owners of the idle building sold their resources to the first bidders, that is, cut their offering prices sufficiently to obtain employment immediately. From the standpoint of economic efficiency as well as that of utility maximization by the resource owners, it is worthwhile (up to a point) to hold

---

[2] And good company treasurers rent out most of their unused cash balances for periods as short as a day.

the resources idle and seek information. For the human agent, a rapid sequence of jobs would entail contracting costs, adjustment costs, perhaps the conveyance of damaging information about the individual's capabilities; and it would necessitate foregoing the use of his time to acquire information. For nonhuman resources, the owner would encounter most of these costs also, though the re-contracting costs might be higher and the time sacrificed by putting the resource to work (time that could otherwise be used to acquire information) might be smaller.

Employers behave in the same way as other owners or managers of resources. They often have openings or unfilled jobs for machines or buildings or people, which is tantamount to saying that some of the other resources under their control, including the employer's own talents, are idle or underemployed. It would be a misuse of their resources, however, to hire the first laborer, junior executive, building, or machine that was available. Employers do not have instant costless information about future demand conditions, future cost conditions, the marginal value product of each specific person or building, or the prices they would have to pay for substitute inputs. Even if the employer felt fairly sure that a particular machine or employee would be worth the asking price, it would ordinarily be economical to devote at least a little time to a search for still better alternatives. Hence employers advertise and shop around; they do not make instant offers and commitments. In effect, the employer's idle or underemployed resources *are* "employed" just as the idle resources of other owners are often occupied: in a waiting or search activity that appears to be their best use in the circumstances. These resources are engaged in producing a basket of goods that is preferred to the alternatives.

Suppose one now raises the cost of offering employment to others, or of accepting employment, by introducing not merely ordinary adjustment costs plus uncertainties about the demand for particular resources and the supplies of substitutes but also shifts in demand for entire industries' products. As one firm reduces its output and releases resources, other firms in the industry will be doing so also. The individual resource owner searches for his next-best opportunity, but as he samples the more obvious possibilities, such as other firms in the same industry, he finds that bids for his services there are also declining. Since he does not discover attractive alternatives promptly, he feels that further search is likely to be valuable, and he does not sacrifice as much as he formerly would have sacrificed by searching longer. Going further afield and working in other industries, locations, or occupations, however, will entail heavier moving and adjustment costs. Moreover, despite efforts to acquire information, there will still be comparatively great uncertainties about the prospects, working conditions, and living conditions—in other words, the utility—

associated with these less familiar situations. All these factors will make such options relatively unattractive and make waiting and acquiring more information relatively attractive.

At the same time similar factors are affecting employers in the declining industry. The costs of their inputs are not falling much initially, because the owners of these inputs shift them to other users or shop for information rather than cut their offering prices by whatever amount would be necessary to retain their jobs. This will be as true for buildings, supplies, and raw materials as it is for labor. Sticky prices as well as sticky wages stem from the existence of alternative opportunities and the search for information about them. Consequently, employers must reduce outputs and release resources. Moreover, the decline in demand renders obsolete the information previously possessed by employers about the marginal value products of inputs and about the prices at which they will be able to get various inputs. Employers too will find it advantageous to hold a more than usual amount of their resources "idle," avoid adjustment costs, and seek information.

Now imagine that a decline in aggregate demand occurs. The effects of adjustment and information costs are now multiplied. Suppose the decline is first observed in the retail sector. Retailers first see inventories piling up; the prices charged by wholesalers, suppliers, and labor have not changed. Most input owners choose to shop around rather than chop their offering prices immediately. The store owners reduce their orders from wholesalers and may release some clerks or other resources. Wholesalers too are ignorant of the shift and any impending shifts in consumers' demands for goods. All they see initially is accumulation of their inventories. Cost conditions for them have not changed; they cut their orders from manufacturers and reduce output. As output declines, marginal costs presumably go down somewhat, and these firms will reduce prices somewhat, but they will have released resources. Manufacturers and servicing industries in turn behave similarly.

Owners of released resources seek information about alternative opportunities. Even when they turn to other industries, they find that openings are less attractive than they had expected. Other released resources are out shopping also, and the offering prices of various substitutable inputs begin to fall. Employers, initially caught between declining demand for their products and sticky input prices, now find input prices declining but also find it worthwhile to seek information about the prices they must pay for inputs as well as about prices they can obtain for outputs. They reduce commitments, release resources, wait, and shop for information.

As more resources are held idle, the incomes and wealth of the owners decline, pessimistic expectations are generated, people tighten their belts still further, and aggregate demand falls still more. As the downward spiral continues, previously acquired information becomes obsolete.[3] The effect is similar to the effect that would be observed if all houses suddenly had a life-span of only one month. At the new cost per period, people would demand fewer houses and lower-quality housing, but more resources would be required to produce any given amount of housing accommodation. Similarly, people settle for lower-quality information about demand and supply conditions during a deflation, but more and more effort is required to produce a given amount of such information. Simultaneously the options that do appear—perhaps, at the extreme, selling apples on the corner—are unattractive, thus reducing the sacrifice entailed by waiting and searching. Confronted with the facts that demands for resources are declining and unpredictable, that information is valuable yet not free or long-lived, and that adjustments are costly yet often of unknown worth, employers and resource owners find prolonged waiting and searching better than the alternatives. (If information were instantly and costlessly available and moving or adjustment costs were zero, everything would have fallen into place instantaneously, and there would have been no "involuntary" unemployment. In our world, however, information and mobility are not costless.)

Thus owners and managers of idle resources are actually putting them to the use that is preferred *in these circumstances*. This is not to say that these resource owners are happy about it or that everything is all right or that the government should merely provide more employment offices or information exchanges! For the preferred or best use of resources in this situation is none too good and can almost certainly be improved upon by altering the circumstances. Some of the possibilities will be considered later. In general, policies to reduce the fluctuations of aggregate demand and the explosion of information and adjustment costs would seem to be indicated. One should not move along those lines regardless of cost, however, as military or central planning sometimes seems to do. One would not wish, for example, to eliminate change in order to cut adjustment costs, to produce goods and services for people without regard for their preferences, to assign resources without regard for information about their worth in alternative uses, or simply to call resources employed and send checks to their owners indefinitely even if the resources were in fact idle.

Incidentally, secular changes in employment, as well as changes associated with fluctuations of aggregate demand, deserve a word of explanation. According to many observers, there has been in recent years an increase in the average rate of unemployment even during prosperity. Estimates are made by taking

---

[3] The belt tighteners and indeed all participants in the process are inflicting external costs on others, a major aspect of which is the increased information and adjustment costs thrust upon each other.

surveys at particular points in time and determining what percentage of the samples are unemployed. All unemployed individuals are not permanently idle, of course. Most are between jobs, but if each such person spends more time than he formerly did in looking for his next position, a larger percentage of persons will be unemployed at any point in time.

Information and adjustment costs are involved here too, along with any factors that make "idleness" or search more or less expensive. With innovation and rapid change, more reshuffling of resources becomes appropriate, and with information and adjustment costs, more time will be spent between jobs in search activities. With changing barriers to entry—for example, with Negroes acquiring access to new occupations, with some unions or oligopolies gaining power and restricting entry and others losing power—resource shifts will occur, and because of information and adjustment costs, the process will yield idle resources. At the same time affluence may make people willing to devote more time to leisure and search than they formerly did; these may be more pleasant activities, and the marginal utility of income may be less, than they formerly were. Then, too, higher tax rates and more generous welfare programs make unemployment less expensive to the unemployed than it used to be.[4] If unemployment rates do show a secular rise, it is hardly an inexplicable phenomenon.

causes of changes in aggregate spending

So much for the effects, in the light of information and adjustment costs, of changes in aggregate spending. Before asking what public spending policies might be adopted, let us inquire into the causes of the fluctuations in aggregate demand. As noted earlier, total spending per period is determined by the choices of millions of utility maximizers. What factors can make an increment or decrement in spending relatively attractive to these individuals?

In trying to answer this question, many persons, whether or not they agree with Keynes' views on public spending policy, believe that his analytical framework is useful. In this scheme, total spending is broken down into consumption, investment, and government purchases. Higher net incomes are assumed to move consumers to spend more; lower interest rates and higher incomes are often assumed to induce greater spending for investment; and government purchases are exogenously determined by policy makers. Other variables are sometimes introduced, but in the main the models suggest that one can increase aggregate demand by cutting taxes, expanding government purchases, or

---

[4] Though this unemployment would show up partly in the form of withdrawals from the labor force.

lowering interest rates. The precise effects of a particular action depend upon the estimated relationships among these variables. And the effects include repercussions on foreign trade and thence on domestic spending.

Other persons have focused attention on the stock of money, arguing that utility maximizers will trade more money for goods, that is, spend more, if the value of their money supply is increased relative to the value of their other assets. This relationship or model, which comprises various versions of the "quantity theory of money," suggests that one can increase aggregate demand by expanding the stock of money, the precise effects depending upon the estimated relationship. In the most extreme version, the only time that government spending could increase total demand would be when the government's action expanded the supply of money, as would happen if the government ran a deficit and financed it with new money.

Both of these models have received harsh criticism. It has been pointed out that the usual Keynesian model neglects factors, such as the stock of money, that would certainly seem to influence utility maximizers significantly. It took a surprising amount of time for most economists to see another major qualification: that consumption is not likely to have a stable relationship to income during a particular period, though it might have such a relationship to "permanent income." After all, if one's income soars (or slumps) to $1,000 for July only, his rate of spending is not likely to change as much as it would if he anticipated receiving $1,000 per month indefinitely.

Critics of the quantity theory of money, on the other hand, have insisted that total spending varies for many reasons other than changes in the stock of money—declaring, at the extreme, that the velocity of circulation has no stability at all or, in other words, that the size of people's cash balances has no impact on their spending decisions. And it does indeed appear that velocity varies, not only temporarily but also secularly, depending upon such variables as interest rates, expectations about prices, the cost of using checking accounts, and the supply of money substitutes. That velocity has no stability, however, appears to be far from the truth.

Like other models, the Keynesian and quantity-theory models abstract from much of reality. This is quite appropriate; a set of relationships that even approximately mirrored reality would not facilitate one's thinking about aggregate demand more than would a detailed photograph of the entire nation. At the same time, though, one must not lose sight of the fact that these models are merely analytical devices. One could develop thousands of them. For example, one could break total spending down into spending on crackerjacks C, making it a function of income, and all other spending I, making it an exogenous variable. For equilibrium to exist, intended total spending would have to equal intended total income.[5] This set of relationships would predict the equilibrium level of income, given perturbations in *I* or in the crackerjack function. A parody on the quantity-theory model might be as follows. Spending *PT* could be broken down into the dollar value of government bonds *B* and velocity of circulation (*PT* divided by *B*). If one assumes that velocity is constant and introduces the equilibrium condition that intended *BV* must equal intended *PT*, one has a predictive model.

But these models, whether absurd or plausible, are not tested hypotheses. Until implications are spelled out and checked against observations in the real world, these analytical devices are merely gadgets to assist thinking. Moreover —presumably because hypothesis testing is difficult, time-consuming, and often relatively unrewarding from the standpoint of professional advancement—more effort seems to flow into the building of models than into the checking of hypotheses. In the empirical work that has been done so far, the stock of liquid assets does appear to be a crucial variable in shaping total spending (though velocity of circulation is not a constant).[6] And government deficits, which produce increases in both disposable income and the supply of liquid assets, usually seem to generate higher total expenditures. Beyond this, our beliefs are on none too firm a base. Economists have learned much less about these matters during the past three decades than many people imagine. Additional effort to test propositions would yield value in the form of increased knowledge. Of course, additional effort to formulate models *and the implications of models* would also yield such value if designed specifically for empirical verification rather than just for mental exercise.

government spending and fluctuations

For the government to do nothing that affects the economy is practically ruled out. Through political and bureaucratic processes, decisions are made that affect the stock of money, total tax receipts, and the volume of government spending. Moreover, these variables will be manipulated deliberately in an effort to influ-

---

[5] See the Appendix at the end of Chapter 6 for a clarification of the function of an equilibrium condition versus the irrelevance of an identity. Even today there is a surprising amount of confusion about this matter.

[6] Milton Friedman and Anna J. Schwartz, *A Monetary History of the United States 1867–1960*, National Bureau of Economic Research, Princeton University Press, Princeton, N.J., 1963. For tests of hypotheses about the determinants of the money supply, see Karl Brunner and Allan H. Meltzer, *An Alternative Approach to the Monetary Mechanism*, House Committee on Banking and Currency, Subcommittee on Domestic Finance, 88th Cong., 2d Sess., 1964.

ence fluctuations (and they will also be manipulated inadvertently). Utility maximization by officials, legislators, and voters will now see to that. In the light of all this, what public spending policies are likely to be considered and what is known about their consequences?

kinds of action

If deflation threatens, central governments are almost certain nowadays to turn to deficit financing, and this in turn will increase disposable incomes and the stock of liquid assets in the hands of households and firms, in comparison with what that stock would otherwise have been. The extent of the increase in liquidity depends upon how the deficit is financed, but to the extent that the central banks end up holding more bonds, new money is injected into the economy (see the later section on debt). Deficits will be created automatically by decreases in tax receipts as incomes decline and by increases in welfare payments as more persons become eligible for unemployment and other welfare benefits. In addition, if the deflation is severe, political forces are likely to lead to reductions in tax rates or increases in spending programs.

Despite the dearth of tested hypotheses, most persons would probably agree that such steps will increase total spending. Even this much was apparently not believed widely during the Great Depression, for the alignment of political pressures did not lead to much deficit spending and money injection in the early and middle thirties. Nowadays, partly because of this change in knowledge, political forces would surely lead to large deficits and money injections in the United States and probably in most nations—*if* it became clear that the country was in a major deflation.

If inflation threatens, it is not as clear what governments would do. The recent growth in knowledge about inflation may not have been as great as that about deflation, for it was presumably believed long ago that to halt runaway inflation it was necessary to stop the rapid expansion of the money supply and that this could be done by running a surplus and "retiring" money from circulation. Whether or not convictions are stronger than they used to be about the way to stop inflations, utility-maximizing officials are less certain to develop surpluses and retire money during inflation than they are to develop deficits and inject money during deflations. The costs to officials and legislators of achieving surpluses and putting the money on ice are likely to be relatively great and the rewards relatively small (though these costs and rewards depend upon voters' and colleagues' interests, and in some circumstances the attitudes of strong coalitions could upset this conclusion).

effects that are still unknown

As noted above, there has occurred an important change in the state of knowledge about coping with deflation. At the same time, the extent of our ignorance about the precise impacts of alternative policies is startling. There is little basis for complacent statements that major depressions will never occur again. There is considerable agreement about the *kind* of action that would stimulate aggregate spending, but very little agreement, unless a deep depression exists, about *whether* aggregate spending should be stimulated or *how much* it should be stimulated, and little understanding about *how much government action* would produce a specified increase in total spending. The reasons are that little is known (1) about what other shifts in aggregate demand are about to take place (ask yourself at any particular moment whether total spending is about to rise or fall, or whether stockmarket averages are about to rise or fall), (2) about the quantitative impact of specified deficits and money injections on total spending, and (3) about the lags between the various steps involved in taking action and the timing of the impacts on demand.

Many other effects, such as impacts on the balance of payments and relations with other nations, are highly uncertain. Consider the alternative policies of financing either half or two-thirds of a deficit by selling bonds to the central bank, or, as another example, the alternative policies of achieving the deficit by cutting taxes only or partly by cutting taxes and partly by increasing expenditures: the differences in the effects are not known with any precision. With the consequences only dimly understood, policy makers have abundant room for disagreement; lengthy debates and delays are understandable; and final actions are predictable in only the vaguest fashion. For these reasons, too, there is little basis for complacency about what utility-maximizing members of a body politic will in fact do and therefore about what the consequences will really be.

rules versus discretion

Because of such uncertainties, and also because of the advantages of dispersed authority (see Chapter 2 on the unseen hand in government and Chapter 7 on freedom), many persons have advocated heavy reliance on predetermined rules about monetary-fiscal actions rather than on discretionary authority. Most persons want some constraints or guidelines spelled out ahead of time, and some, like Henry Simons, have urged virtually complete specification of the rules in advance.[7] The case for rules is like the case for adopting any rule of thumb—namely, the belief that the gains would outweigh the costs. Advocates of rules are keenly aware that individuals are utility maximizers, and they believe that, with much discretion, utility-maximizing officials would adopt even worse policies, from the standpoint of other individuals, than rules would produce. They visualize policies that would be worse in terms of predictability and stabilization and also in terms of the concentration of power and the deterioration of the bargaining mechanism.

As for specific types of rules, there are numerous possibilities. One would be to require a steady expansion of the money stock, say 3 or 5 percent a year, with the money stock carefully defined and with specified adjustments required every week. In addition, if unemployment as it is measured exceeded, say, 6 percent of the labor force, specified cuts in tax rates and specified additional injections of money could be prearranged. Such rules could be designed at leisure instead of in haste, could shield officials from the conflicting pressures and doubts that beset them during crises, could reduce the instability of anticipations by households and business firms, and could decrease the extent of arbitrary power possessed by officials.

Many economists, however, are skeptical about extreme reliance on automatic rules. They point out that "mild" rules, such as our automatic stabilizers today, tend to damp down but not reverse fluctuations in aggregate demand, and might therefore be labeled "automatic tranquilizers" rather than stabilizers.[8] Skeptics also point out that one has to cope with the uncertainties mentioned above in designing and setting up rules, just as someone has to cope with these uncertainties in shaping discretionary policies. In other words, one does not avoid our ignorance about lags, forecasts of other events, quantitative impacts of monetary-fiscal actions, and political processes by turning to rules. Moreover, most rules, it might be argued, would themselves require centralization of authority even if the new repository were not a person. That is, authority would in effect be taken from the Federal Reserve Board, the Treasury, the Congress, and so on and placed in the hands of an impersonal book of rules, which might have unanticipated repercussions on the bargaining process and the centralization of authority. (In fact, since the constraints and specifications would be legislation, such rules would be only temporarily inviolable, and discretion would be retained by the legislative body instead of being delegated to an authority.) Finally, it is often pointed out that the adoption of rigid rules in advance would

---

[7] Henry C. Simons, "Rules Versus Authorities in Monetary Policy," *Journal of Political Economy*, February, 1936, pp. 1–30; reprinted in Henry C. Simons, *Economic Policy for a Free Society*, The University of Chicago Press, Chicago, 1948.

[8] Walter W. Heller, "CED's Stabilizing Budget Policy After Ten Years," *American Economic Review*, September, 1957, pp. 634–651.

entail the sacrifice of later and better information as particular fluctuations occurred.

Some of the arguments on both sides of the rules-versus-discretion question are impressive. The use of rules probably obeys the usual laws of economics. Beyond some point, additional units of any input or adaptation bring diminishing returns; and there is rarely such a thing as "free lunch." But there are few tested hypotheses about the use of rules versus discretion; there is little firm knowledge about the costs and gains from alternative arrangements. In my own judgment, it would be wise to employ a monetary-expansion rule, perhaps combined with provisions for additional injections via tax cuts if serious danger signals appeared. Or tax cuts might be partly left to the discretion of the executive branch of the government *in specified circumstances and up to specified limits*. If such rules were tried, it would be imperative for everyone to realize that large amounts of money are involved. (It would be unwise to adopt a rule that tried to prime the pump with a medicine dropper; when that failed, people might easily elect to have the government run the pump.) Three percent of U.S. gross national product in the mid-sixties is about $20 billion. A rule to expand the money supply by 5 percent per year would involve injections, such as deficits financed by created money, of $7 or $8 billion per year. One should not blanch at the thought. As Paul Getty is said to have remarked when he estimated he was worth several billion dollars: "But you have to remember that a billion today isn't what a billion used to be!"

tax cuts versus expenditure increases

If government tries to inaugurate large new spending programs to counter a deflation, there is likely to be considerable delay and waste, even if the spending projects are planned and placed on the shelf ahead of time. Tax cuts, on the other hand, can nowadays yield relatively prompt and predictable injections, and the individuals who are made wealthier can be counted on to make reasonably efficient[9] expenditure choices. For such reasons, many economists argue that public expenditures should be chosen on the basis of their merits, and that tax variations and bond purchases or sales should be the main monetary-fiscal tools employed to counter fluctuations. But these and other points about tax cuts versus expenditure increases are commonplace.[10] Only a point that may be *comparatively* neglected will be stressed here.

---

[9] Efficient in the usual Paretian sense.

[10] There are many good discussions of the alternative routes to injecting purchasing power into an economy. For an early treatment, see W. H. Beveridge, *Full Employment in a Free Society*, W. W. Norton & Company, Inc., New York, 1945. For a modern summary, see Armen A. Alchian and William R. Allen, *University Economics*, 2d ed., Wadsworth Publishing Co., Inc., Belmont, Calif., 1967, pp. 623–635.

This point is that utility maximization by legislators, officials, and voters is likely to produce a ratchet effect if expenditure increases are used to combat successive deflations. That is, the decision-making process is likely to yield a succession of expenditure increases rather than increases during deflations that are cut back after the deflations are over. In other words, one consequence of using expenditure increases to combat recessions is an increased probability of further expansion, for outlays tend to be ratcheted upward instead of being moved up and then back down. This would happen, not because anyone is power-mad or anxious to have government expand, but because ratcheting outlays upward is *relatively* rewarding behavior for most of the individual participants in the process.[11]

The effect is most clearly seen when expenditures and taxes are raised during wars. Afterward, budgets rarely drop back to prewar levels. At least part of the tax revenues are retained and reallocated to other programs.[11] The reason is that, like anyone else, public officials always have valuable things in mind that they would like to do. It is relatively costly to these persons to ask Congress to levy new taxes but relatively inexpensive to ask for a reallocation of funds from a declining program or from tax revenues that are already there. This is true because congressmen ordinarily find it relatively costly in terms of votes to levy new taxes but relatively inexpensive to use taxes that are already being collected. Information, adjustment, and decision-making costs to the voter are lower if the taxes already exist.

What happens if government expenditures are raised, and tax rates are left unchanged, when deflation strikes? As recovery occurs, tax receipts increase. It is less expensive to voters, officials, and legislators to put these receipts into programs—to maintain government expenditures—than it would be if tax rates had been cut and tax receipts after recovery were lower. This is not to say that there will *never* be expenditure cuts or that countercyclical policy is the only variable affecting the size of government outlays or that the ratchet is 100 percent effective. But it is to say that increasing public expenditures is rendered less costly to most participants than it would otherwise be and that the participants will demand more government activities at this "lower price."

Is this bad? Not necessarily. It depends upon one's judgments about the various effects. Some possible undesirable impacts are discussed in Chapter 7 on the connections between public spending and individual freedom. Markedly increased government outlays may make more persons beholden to government officials, and it is usually undesirable for too many to owe too much to too few.

---

[11] See Alan T. Peacock and Jack Wiseman, *The Growth of Public Expenditure in the United Kingdom*, National Bureau of Economic Research, New York, 1961; and James M. Buchanan, *Public Finance in Democratic Process: Fiscal Institutions and Individual Choice*, The University of North Carolina Press, Chapel Hill, N.C., 1967.

Some related consequences, stemming from the possible relationships between large spending and centralization within government, are examined in Chapters 9 and 10. But, on the other hand, public spending can bring gains or desirable consequences too, and the net effect depends upon the starting point, the circumstances, and one's values. On this issue, one must rely mainly on his judgments, for there are few tested hypotheses here. *If* one wishes to put an additional brake on public spending, however, one should probably advocate tax reductions rather than expenditure increases as antideflation tools.[12] (Whether one's advocacy would have much effect again depends on many variables.) Tax reductions would impair the upward ratchet mechanism, that is, make increases in public outlays a little more expensive to officials, Congressmen, and voters; and sometimes it might even ratchet outlays downward!

is there a fate worse than debt?

Many people prefer an increased but balanced government budget as the way to stimulate total spending in time of recession, often because they are fearful of the growing Federal debt. Analytical models have led some to believe that an increment in a balanced budget will increase the rate of total spending by approximately the size of that increment. One should remember, however, that these models are simply analytical devices, for not many hypotheses stemming from them have been subjected to proper tests. In fact, it may be that an increased balanced budget gives only a small and fleeting fillip to total spending (or has a zero or even deflationary effect).[13] Misplaced faith in this tool, coupled with the secular increase in unemployment, could lead to misguided demands for more and more government spending. In any event, even if the balanced-budget multiplier is nearly 1.0 and an increased balanced budget provides a large stimulus to total spending, this tool will ratchet public spending up more than would cutting taxes and running a deficit.

In effect many persons apparently believe that increases in the debt—even to permit tax reduction during recession and even if controlled by law rather than by administrators—are more radical than government "elephantiasis" (and/or specific controls). They assume that a $10 billion deficit to inject private purchasing power is more objectionable than a $10 billion expansion of

---

[12] And, as anti-inflation tools, one should consider "repayable surcharges." See Harold M. Somers, "How to Increase Taxes without a Tax Increase," MR-68, Institute of Government and Public Affairs, UCLA (a paper presented at the meeting of the Western Economic Association in August, 1966).

[13] Harold M. Somers, "Federal Expenditure and Economic Stability: The Fallacy of the Balanced Budget," in J. Scherer and J. A. Papke (eds.), *Public Finance and Fiscal Policy*, Houghton Mifflin Company, Boston, 1966, pp. 336–345.

government programs financed by taxes. In brief, many persons are more afraid of debt growth than of government growth. As fluctuations occur over the coming decades, these beliefs could lead toward a thoroughgoing welfare state (sometimes called the farewell state!) even if people did not like the concomitant effects of such a state. It is important, therefore, to consider carefully the nature of the Federal debt and its burdens.

debt held by the federal reserve banks

To know what to fear and what not to fear, one must see the debt for what it really is, and part of it is simply the greenback of the twentieth century. That part comprises the government bonds held by the Federal Reserve banks. At the end of 1965, these amounted to $39 billion. To see why this part of the debt is equivalent to greenbacks, let us examine the steps that produce it. Suppose tax receipts are insufficient to meet expenditures. To meet the deficit, the Treasury issues bonds. Suppose further that it sells these bonds to a Federal Reserve bank. In that event, the bank gives the Treasury a checking account in exchange for the bonds. The bank has a new asset, the bonds, and a new liability, the government's checking deposit. Next the government puts its new checking deposit into circulation by paying bills with it. The Treasury writes checks on the account, and the recipients deposit the checks in their banks. The sum of all checking deposits in the possession of firms and individuals, and hence the total money supply, rises.

Clearly the net effect of the operation is the creation of money. Does it at the same time create a bona fide national debt? To reach an answer, one has to know what the twelve Federal Reserve banks are really like. Nominally, they are owned by their stockholders, who happen to be the member banks in which most people have their checking deposits. For all practical purposes, though, the Federal Reserve banks are a part of the government. The dividends they pay to the member banks are limited by law, earnings in excess of these dividends being at the disposal of the government. The Treasury pays interest to the Federal Reserve banks on the bonds they hold, but later much of the money is handed back. The government owes these banks the amount of the bonds they hold, yet if the banks were to wind up their affairs, their assets (in excess of liabilities) would revert to the government according to law. In this respect, they are central banks, and the bonds they hold are owed by the government to the government.

Federal Reserve policy, it is true, may be formulated independently; it is not necessarily consistent with White House or Treasury views. But when the Federal Reserve banks buy bonds, it is as though the government purchased its own obligations with newly created money. The government's true indebtedness does not increase. The same result would be achieved if the Treasury printed up a batch of currency, deposited it with the Federal Reserve banks, and received a new checking account. Of course interest is not paid on an issue of currency, but then it need not be paid on debt held by a central bank.

Incidentally, the consequences are exactly as described if the Treasury sells the bonds first to the general public, and the Federal Reserve banks subsequently buy them from the people. In that case, and it is in fact the way in which the Federal Reserve banks acquire most of their holdings, the public acts merely as an intermediary. When the Federal Reserve banks hold the bonds, "fiat money" rather than national debt is outstanding.

In former times it was fashionable for kings and governments to get their spending money by means of straightforward, though rather crude, devices— for example, by clipping coins and minting the trimmings, or by shaking coins together in bags and "sweating" off pieces of the money metal. Another method was simply to call in the coinage and "cry it up"—to call a farthing a shilling, as the historian Macaulay put it. As late as the 1930s, a modified form of such devaluation was used in the United States when gold was called in and "cried up." In that instance, President Roosevelt and Secretary of the Treasury Morgenthau determined the gold content of the dollar not by clipping coins but by flipping coins. At least that's the way it happened according to some accounts. For the most part, however, those devices were outmoded by the invention of the printing press. When people became accustomed to handling paper money, governments could meet the payroll simply by running off a fresh batch of currency. But the printing press was abused, and it too fell into disrepute. Modern governments cannot usually add to the money supply by overtly printing more of it. Instead they use this new method—selling bonds to themselves in exchange for checking accounts.

The implications of debt held by central banks are considerably different from those of ordinary debt. It is not that people owe it to themselves. It is simply that this kind of government debt is essentially an issue of money. What should be feared about this? Clearly one should not be afraid of money itself, for it is one of the most useful inventions of all time. Nor should one turn pale at the thought of a rising stock of money, which may take the form of a rising debt (since that is the way the government issues money nowadays). What people should be concerned about is (1) too slow or rapid an increase in the stock of money and (2) discretionary authority over the debt and hence over the money supply. These are the two things that have produced trouble—not the issuance of money but the *discretionary* creation of money by monarchs or governments and issuance *at too fast or too slow a pace*. Regulating this kind of debt (that is, the money supply) in a growing economy is like regulating the food supply of a growing child: further feeding regardless of amount should not be taboo, but too much, or too little, or discretionary authority over the quantity, should be matters of concern.

debt held by general public

What about the rest of the debt? Is the part that is held by private firms and individuals the same thing as money?[14] The answer is No, though these government bonds are "near-moneys." Again let us review the steps that lead to their existence. This time suppose that the government meets a deficit by selling bonds to the general public. John Doe gets the bonds, he sends money to the Treasury, and the government puts the money back in circulation by paying bills. The net result is that the supply of money remains the same, but the supply of bonds in the portfolios of private bondholders goes up. These bonds are highly liquid assets that can be converted to money on short notice. They are therefore money substitutes or near-moneys that make it less costly for the owners to hold lower cash balances. But the evidence to date suggests that these money substitutes do not have nearly the impact on total spending that the same increment in the money stock would have.

Moreover, government indebtedness to domestic firms and individuals does bring genuine burdens. Servicing this debt or paying it off calls for the printing of bonds (debt sold directly to the Federal Reserve banks need involve only phone calls and bookkeeping entries), the keeping of extra records, the levying and collecting of taxes, the disbursing of checks, and so on. These activities not only absorb resources, but the imposition of taxes, and perhaps the disbursing of interest payments, have unneutral effects on incentives and resource allocation. Moreover, levying taxes to service or retire such indebtedness results later in compulsory payments rather than a voluntary purchase of bonds (thus placing a burden on whatever generation makes these payments). Debt issued to the Federal Reserve banks could also result in such payments if (1) it was to be retired by drawing on tax receipts, or (2) it was issued so as to generate inflation, which automatically "taxes" the holders of money and fixed claims. But, if issued to combat deflation and unemployment, debt held by the Federal Reserve banks need not be handled in this fashion. If controlled appropriately, such additions to the money stock can simply remain outstanding.

the national debt and stabilization

In view of these probable effects, it is quite appropriate to be concerned about debt. Borrowing from domestic firms and households may be a useful device

---

[14] Debt held by commercial banks is in still a different hybrid category, but to a considerable extent is like debt held by the general public. Only the two "extremes" will be examined here.

when it is desirable to *reduce* the volume of purchasing power in the public's hands, but it is less than sensational as a part of the tool kit for preventing or repairing deflations.[15] For *that* purpose, borrowing from private firms and individuals is not as effective as alternative ways of financing a deficit, and it does bring genuine burdens. It is hardly wise to increase this kind of debt promiscuously and endlessly. Indebtedness to the Federal Reserve banks is an effective way to finance a deficit so as to stimulate spending, and it need not bring the burdens associated with borrowing from the general public. Needless to say, however, it is hardly wise to increase this kind of debt promiscuously either, for this would be tantamount to expanding the money supply capriciously.[16]

It *would* be valuable to use debt to the Federal Reserve banks, that is, created money, so as to permit taxes to be lower than they would otherwise be and enlarge the money supply at a sensible and steady rate—say 3 percent per year—or perhaps at a faster rate when recession threatens. This would have few of the disadvantages associated with the kinds of intervention that might otherwise be adopted. It would not ratchet expenditures upward the way increases in a balanced budget are likely to do. Unlike intervention in specific sectors of the economy, it would not impair the movement of labor and other resources to new occupations or locations. It would not discourage the readjustment of particular industries called for by growth and change. Indeed it would facilitate the reshuffling of resources that is so essential if people are to reap the fruits of research, innovation, and growth. Note that the exodus of labor from the farm always speeds up during prosperity, not during recession. Still more important, this type of government action would not create "kept" industries or people or accelerate the proliferation of constraints on the choices of individuals. It would merely keep the cash registers ringing and opportunities opening. By resisting this type of intervention, people who are essentially libertarian may in effect be supporting policies that are essentially radical.

To employ national debt in this way, it is important to fear debt—but in a discriminating manner: to perceive the differences between the different kinds of national debt, and to recognize that, like most medicines, additional debt to the Federal Reserve banks is beneficial in some dosages and circumstances yet harmful in others. But *uncritical* fear of government indebtedness—the modern means of creating money—could lead us to a fate worse than debt.

---

[15] In fact the easiest way to reduce the real debt would be to shift it to the Federal Reserve banks (or print money and pay it off) *during* deflations. See Henry C. Simons, "On Debt Policy," *Economic Policy for A Free Society.*

[16] It would clarify matters if the term "debt" were reserved for real indebtedness and if the government obtained its deposits with the Federal Reserve banks only by depositing money (see James M. Buchanan, *The Public Finances*, rev. ed., Richard D. Irwin, Inc., Homewood, Ill., 1965, pp. 380–381). But at present the term "debt" has these quite different meanings.

budgetary tools and fluctuations

This book has stressed that voters, officials, and legislators will take less of an action if it is made more expensive from their individual standpoints. Inferior budgetary formats and procedures can make actions that would otherwise be desirable unnecessarily expensive. They can do this by making helpful information costly to obtain (for example, by requiring heavy sacrifices of time and convenience) or unavailable (that is, infinitely expensive). Similarly, poor tools and procedures can make it relatively costly to build houses and can induce people to demand fewer houses of a specified quality. Devising improved budgetary tools, therefore, may make it less difficult for voters, officials, and legislators to shape spending policies so as to reduce fluctuations in aggregate spending. The effect of improved information would cut the *total* price and presumably increase the quantity of "good decisions" demanded.

At the same time, one should not expect miracles even from vastly improved budgetary tools. The disutility to an official or voter of a stabilizing tax cut or increase *from other standpoints*, the difficulties of forecasting and timing, and many other factors would continue to make appropriate policies very difficult. A great reduction in one small component of cost would not cause a large drop in the total cost or induce a large response. Similarly, an enormous improvement in the shovel would not dramatically reduce the costs of building a house. And one should not expect the sales of an item to soar if the price drops from $100 to $99.

So much by way of precaution. Let us turn now to some alternative budgetary arrangements and their advantages and disadvantages.[17] The administrative budget—the familiar published U.S. budget, for example—is not very helpful in shaping monetary-fiscal policies. One reason is that certain transfer expenditures and fund transactions are omitted from this budget. Another and perhaps even more basic reason is that it does not show, and has never purported to show, the impacts of government actions on the flow of income or the stock of liquidity in the private sector. This budget focuses attention on allocative choices, their individual impacts on authorizations, and the impact of spending choices on total authorizations rather than on near-future cash expenditures, receipts, and liquid-asset injections. Figure 2 brings out rather clearly the major discrepancies between the estimates in the administrative budget and estimates of expenditures during the year ahead. Using monetary-fiscal policy with this document as a guide would be like using an antibiotic with almost no information about the quantity contained in the capsules.

---

[17] For a more complete discussion of these matters, see "Budgetary Concepts: A Symposium," *The Review of Economics and Statistics*, May, 1963, pp. 113–147.

The same thing is true of a program budget, which presents the costs for several years ahead that are implied by choices and collects costs in terms of intermediate government outputs rather than for individual inputs regardless of use. (This budgetary reform will be examined in Chapters 8 and 9.) Like administrative budgets, program budgets are intended mainly to assist decision makers in making managerial and allocative choices rather than in influencing aggregate spending. There is nothing about the program budget as such that would yield improved information about governmental impacts on private-income flows or liquid-asset holdings. Accrual accounting and accrual budgets could show impending receipts from and disbursements to the private sector, but because of the almost inevitable delays in collecting such data, the net gain from such modifications would be negligible. Besides, it appears to be

FIG. 2   The relation of authorizations to expenditures

The administrative budget

$ Billions

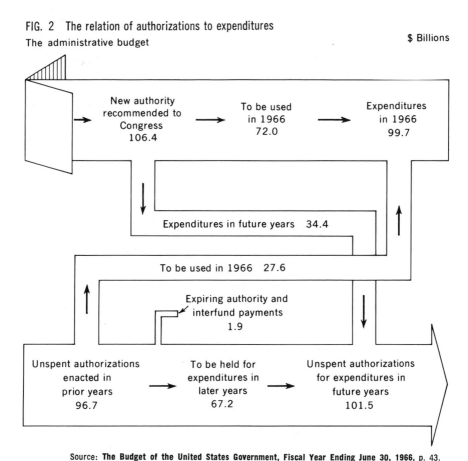

Source: **The Budget of the United States Government, Fiscal Year Ending June 30, 1966, p. 43.**

more important to include all *types* of disbursements and receipts than to include accruals of items in, say, the existing administrative budget.

The once-popular idea of having a capital budget has lost much of its appeal even for its original purposes, such as segregating investment projects to facilitate choosing among the alternatives, to emphasize that part of public spending goes for capital formation, and to justify government borrowing. It no longer seems particularly helpful to segregate such outlays, at least in the Federal government. Many other outlays, such as those for health or education, are capital-forming just as much as electric power projects are. Moreover, current welfare or operating outlays are often close substitutes for investment projects. Comparisons should not be confined to alternatives within a capital budget, and it does not seem wise to do anything that might introduce a bias in favor of tangible investment projects. In any event, capital budgets contribute virtually nothing to the formulation of monetary-fiscal decisions. In the depth of the Great Depression, they might have reduced the psychic costs of borrowing from the Federal Reserve banks and injecting money, but in this day and age they do nothing to make the right kind of debt less costly in the eyes of voters and officials at the right times.

A recently popular budgetary suggestion—a National Income and Product Account (NIPA) budget—also has little to offer. The unmodified NIPA budget reflects accruals and would exclude financial transactions: the purchase and sale of mortgages, other financial assets, and used assets. Since these transactions have important impacts on the liquidity position of the private sector, they should hardly be omitted from an exhibit that is supposed to assist monetary-fiscal decisions.

This brings one to the Cash Budget, a *complete* statement of cash expenditures and cash receipts that could be reconciled with both the administrative budget and, if desired, the national income and product accounts.[18] Together with an exhibit showing the way in which deficits or surpluses are to be financed and the way this would affect liquid-asset holdings, the cash budget provides the kind of information that may make appropriate decisions less costly to officials, legislators, and voters. To repeat, however, this probably provides only a very slight reduction in the difficulty of reaching improved monetary-fiscal rules or actions. Budgetary format and procedure is only one of many variables affecting the costs and rewards from decisions that affect aggregate spending. At any one moment, people focus their attention on one particular variable, and they often greatly exaggerate its significance, somewhat as did each of the blind men when he felt a part of the elephant.

---

[18] For more detail see *ibid.*, especially Otto Eckstein, "On Choice of Concepts for the Federal Budget," pp. 126–131.

what is the correct policy?

It may be advisable at this point to emphasize once again that there is no ultimately correct policy in group decision making—unless there is unanimous agreement on a specific policy. In connection with monetary-fiscal policy, each voter and government officeholder will decide what policy he prefers on the basis of the impacts on a host of elements in his utility function. These impacts will include what he believes each policy will do to the price level and employment, to his personal wealth, to international relations, to the incentives of other taxpayers, to the probability that government will become larger, to the probability that individual rights (particularly his) will be impaired, to the probability that the bargaining process or institutional framework in government will be altered, to the incentives and behavior of transfer-payment recipients, and so on. Each person will seek, with the aid of various value judgments and degrees of perception, to maximize his utility—that is, to seek preferredness.

Needless to say, there will be disagreement. What then would be a correct policy from the "standpoint of the nation"? It is impossible to identify any such policy. Suppose A prefers a rule that would yield deficits in specified circumstances, B prefers a balanced-budget rule, and C prefers that officials have discretionary authority. To obtain the other benefits of majority rule, they may agree to abide by this rule (or alternatively to delegate all decisions to A). Or they may just fight and find out in that way who is right about the matter. But there is no ultimate test of preferredness from the group's viewpoint, even in decisions about monetary-fiscal policy.

appendix

TO CHAPTER SIX

identities versus equilibrium conditions

So much emphasis has at times been given to the fact that actual savings must always equal actual investment that, although the subject is an old one, it still seems to generate confusion. Identities such as $S \equiv I$ are completely irrelevant to predictive models, though they may help one see what happens moment by moment in period analysis.

Consider first the familiar predictive model based on supply-and-demand curves or schedules. The supply schedule is a list of quantities that will be offered for sale at various prices. They are "intended," not actual, quantities to be sold. The demand schedule is a list of quantities that will be demanded at various prices. They are "intended," not actual, quantities to be bought. The equilibrium

---

Note: For the first and clearest exposition of these points that I know of, see Jacob Marschak, "Identity and Stability in Economics: A Survey," *Econometrica*, January, 1942, pp. 61–74.

condition is that the intended quantity bought equal the intended quantity sold. In algebraic terms:

$$Q_s = f(p)$$
$$Q_b = f(p)$$
$$Q_s = Q_b \qquad \text{(equilibrium condition)}$$

This set of relationships constitutes a determinate system and a predictive model.

It is quite unnecessary to make use of any identity. It is irrelevant, though true, that the actual quantity bought will always equal the actual quantity sold. An act of selling by one person is automatically an act of buying by someone else. Suppose the price is controlled and is set at a level below the intersection of the demand and supply curves. The "intended or scheduled quantity bought" will exceed the "intended or scheduled quantity sold," and there will be a disequilibrium. Needless to say, however, the actual quantity bought will be identical with the actual amount sold. There are many other situations in which departures from the equilibrium position will occur, that is, situations in which there will be unintended sales or nonsales and unintended purchases or nonpurchases. Suppose supply conditions change suddenly, and the price goes up. Customers do not make their complete response immediately. Buyers must seek information about substitutes and their prices. The husband shopping for groceries may say, "Well, I'll buy the amount my wife wanted this time, and then find out how she wishes to adjust." Furthermore, sellers may at times encounter a surprisingly high demand and run out of stock, selling less than they are willing to sell, or they may draw down their inventories, selling more (for the sake of goodwill) than they intended at a particular price. These things, too, happen because instant costless information is not available. The result is a disequilibrium situation in which scheduled amounts sold do not equal scheduled amounts bought. But *actual* quantities sold will equal *actual* quantity bought.

One could adapt the model to these facts by changing the supply-and-demand curves moment by moment to reflect the adaptability of the suppliers and demanders. And indeed it is common to distinguish between long-run and short-run response by using different curves that reflect the greater degree of adaptability that exists if longer periods of time are available for adaptation. Except in period analysis, however, supply-and-demand curves are not revised moment by moment. Moreover, in order to predict anything, these models must not consist of identities saying in effect that "Whatever happens, happens." They must employ scheduled or intended relationships and equilibrium conditions saying that if a certain price does not exist, there will be disequilibrium, i.e., departures from the intended or planned behavior, that will yield further adaptations pushing toward the equilibrium situation.

Similarly, in Keynesian models, the investment schedule or curve shows, not actual investment at different income levels, but the amounts of investment I that would be intended at various income levels; and the savings schedule or curve shows the amounts of saving S that would be intended at alternative income levels Y. The third relationship that makes this a determinate system is a condition for the existence of equilibrium—namely, that intended savings equal intended investment. For example, if we assume that investment does not vary at all with income level, we could have:

$$I = k \quad \text{(a constant)}$$
$$S = f(Y)$$
$$I = S \quad \text{(equilibrium condition)}$$

It is not only unnecessary but also misleading to employ an identity. To be sure, it is true that actual investment (the difference between total output and actual consumption) is identical with actual saving (the difference between total income and actual consumption). It is true because actual total output is identical to actual total income. An act of saving by one person is automatically an act of investing or dissaving by someone. Suppose you save $10; then either someone's inventories are $10 higher than they would otherwise have been (matching the saving with investment) or someone's income, and momentary saving, is $10 less than it would otherwise have been (matching the saving with dissaving). It should also be noted that an act of investment by one person is automatically matched by an act of saving or disinvesting by someone. Suppose you add $10 worth of investment to a factory you are building. If the $10 is paid to a laborer, he either saves it, which matches the investment, or spends it, which reduces someone's inventories and matches the investment with disinvestment. If the $10 is paid for supplies or raw materials, it reduces someone's inventories and matches the investment with disinvestment. Whatever the events and their sequence, actual investment will always equal actual savings.

But scheduled or intended investment and scheduled saving are the variables that are relevant to predicting behavior in this model of income determination. Only at equilibrium are they equal, and as long as there are departures from scheduled investment or saving, individuals will keep adjusting their behavior.

Consider, for example, the following diagram. If the investment schedule rises by CD, that is, from I to I', income is supposed to increase from OA to OB. It will not do so instantaneously, however, because of lags in adjustments by households and producers. These lags are due in turn to information and

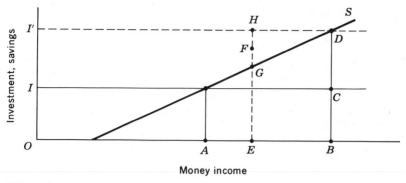

FIG. 3   Determinants of the equilibrium level of income

adjustment costs. If there is unemployment, part of the increment in investment, CD, becomes income to laborers and owners of other inputs. (If there were no unemployment, a different sequence of steps would ensue, illustrating the same point but in a different way.) Recipients will not respond immediately by spending the scheduled percentage of this income. Indeed in the first day after its receipt, the marginal propensity to consume may be nearly zero. Only as the recipients acquire information and adjust will the marginal propensity to consume take on its "normal," "scheduled," or "intended" value. In the meantime some abnormal, unplanned, unscheduled, or unintended savings will occur. Another part of the increment in investment CD is used to purchase goods and results in a reduction in inventories of cement, machinery, thumbtacks, and so on. Moreover, as the income recipients previously mentioned do spend part of their new incomes, the immediate result is a reduction in inventories (compared with what they would otherwise have been). Retailers and dealers, deciding to restore their desired inventory levels, transmit orders to wholesalers and thence to manufacturers, whose inventories are in turn reduced. Thus, the initial effects include unintended or unscheduled disinvestments. Only when manufacturers increase production and scheduled inventories are restored (and the subsequent repercussions are adjusted to) can the economy get back to the investment schedule.

During the disequilibrium period, there must be deviations from the schedules or curves. At one point, for example, the rate of income might actually be OE, and the rates of actual saving and actual investment might be EF. Unscheduled or unintended savings would make actual savings (EF) greater than scheduled savings (EG) from income OE, and unscheduled or unintended disinvestment would make actual investment (EF) less than scheduled investment (EH). There would be forces pushing toward the equilibrium position, however, as householders acquired information and adjusted to get back to the savings schedule and as firms acquired information and adjusted to get back to the investment schedule. Note that actual (i.e., observed, measurable, ex post, realized) saving *EF* would equal actual investment *EF* and that this fact is completely irrelevant to the Keynesian predictive model.

Precisely the same thing is true in connection with the quantity theory of money. In its most elementary form, for instance, the determinate system or predictive model is that intended velocity *V* equals a constant and that, at equilibrium, scheduled *MV* (quantity of money times velocity of circulation) equals scheduled total spending *PT*:

$$M = c \qquad \text{(a given amount)}$$
$$V = K \qquad \text{(a constant)}$$
$$MV = PT \qquad \text{(equilibrium condition)}$$

It is true, of course, that actual *MV* will always be equal to *PT*, but, like all identities, it is consistent with everything and predicts nothing. It is the condition that, if equilibrium is to exist, scheduled *MV* must equal scheduled *PT* that gives the model the ability to predict the volume of total spending (or, with the addition of an equation regarding *T*, the price level).

This distinction between identities or tautologies and predictive models is pertinent to many other applications of economic analysis—for example, models concerning the balance of payments. All these analytical devices would have been easier to understand if identities had never been mentioned. As a case in point, the identity between quantity bought and quantity sold is rarely mentioned, and the way supply-and-demand curves determine an equilibrium price is relatively clear to students. Given the fact that identities *have* been mentioned in connection with Keynesian models, however, it is important to perceive the distinction between them and equilibrium conditions and to see the irrelevance of the identities.

seven

LARGE-SCALE PUBLIC SPENDING AND FREEDOM

As noted before, public spending is capable of producing numerous important effects—some that most persons would regard as desirable, others that they would regard as undesirable. So far, there has been little mention of one of the most significant effects of government spending—namely, its impact on the freedom and rights of individuals. It is so difficult to speak with any assurance on this topic that it is tempting to put the issue aside and "let George write about it." But it is such an important matter, compared to, say, efficiency in producing conventional goods and services, that even a tiny improvement in our understanding here may be worth considerable trouble. I have therefore decided to explore the possible impacts of public spending on freedom, even though what is said does not carry one very far.

I shall assume here that wider range of choice is better than a narrower one, though it is impossible to show just how generally this is true. (Sometimes one may experience a certain amount of agony in choosing and may attach positive value to having certain options foreclosed.) This discussion will pertain mainly to the ranges of choice involved in such basic individual rights as freedom of speech, press, worship, assembly, and voting. Some expenditures, such as those to provide an acceptable, though inevitably imperfect, system of law and order and contract enforcement, work toward protecting these rights. Without those government programs, might would tend to be right, and most minority groups and individuals would fare poorly. Thus some government activities are unquestionably powerful forces to promote the freedom of ordinary individuals. It is often contended, however, that the growth of other government activities is a threat to their liberty. This is a most serious issue, for the flavor of life depends crucially on the options that individuals have in speaking, worshiping, writing, moving about, choosing jobs, and so on, especially in relation to the options they feel are technically possible.

What do government expenditures really have to do with freedom? Plenty of assertions have been made in answer to this question. Hayek and many others say that large government programs lead to serfdom. Sometimes assertions are buttressed by metaphors:

> As I have mentioned before, this is the Achilles heel which is an ideal entrance for the massive Federal octopus because the current civil rights and poverty climate tailors itself perfectly for Federal invasion of the public education field at the local level in these areas. Of course it will be said that "we only want to help in these specific areas" but soon the full blown tiger is in your tank.[1]

Others say, "Well, how has big government impaired your freedom lately? Do many persons in the United States or Great Britain feel less free today than they did several decades ago?" Actually, appallingly little is known about the connection between public spending and liberty.[2] There are inherently great uncertainties about this connection. Furthermore, people have seemingly been content with assertions about the matter and have seldom employed an analytical framework to try to sharpen their intuitive judgments about it. Here, after a fairly lengthy background discussion, I shall try to use economic theory to improve at least slightly our understanding of the connection between public expenditures and freedom.

Most people would agree that there are, inevitably, abridgments of individuals' freedoms—that inevitably there are instances of compulsion in which certain individuals or groups are given less freedom along certain lines so that they may have more of other things, or are restricted in their freedoms so that others may have a greater range of choice. Any activity supported by taxes compels some groups to give up resources for purposes they might not volun-

---

[1] From *The Congressional Record*, quoted in *The New Yorker*, Oct. 31, 1964, p. 202.
[2] This view is expressed, for example, by both Francis M. Bator, *The Question of Government Spending*, Harper and Row, Publishers, Incorporated, New York, 1960, chap. 8; and George J. Stigler, "Reflections on Liberty" (unpublished manuscript).

tarily support. Frequently, however, an effort has been made to render certain basic freedoms or rights—such as worship, assembly, press, or speech—widely available. In this connection, it might be noted that free speech or assembly does not mean "free resources," for if one person uses an acre of ground, an hour of television time, or a speaking platform for his purpose, he prevents someone else from devoting that resource to another purpose, unless the resource is so abundant as to be a free good. For this reason, the basic freedoms have never meant—and should never mean—that people have the right to use just any properties, whether privately or publicly owned, for assembly or worship or public speaking. These basic freedoms mean that each person has the right to buy or rent a site via voluntary exchange and speak or worship there freely without fear of criminal prosecution. Even then, of course, the activity has to be conducted without disturbing the peace or violating the rights of others, and borderline cases can easily arise. Additional abridgments of freedom by government (as well as those imposed by nature) are likely to become more numerous as population densities, urbanization, and interdependencies increase. In effect, most persons will regard it as economical to trade some freedom for additional amounts of other outputs.

For the most part the concern here will be with the links, if any, between government spending and these basic rights. To be sure, freedom to choose among alternative goods or services is an aspect of liberty. The impairment of one's ability to choose freely from the full range of goods that are technologically possible is often exceedingly frustrating, and certainly the degree of choice in this respect is important. I prefer, however, to count consumers' freedom or sovereignty as part of the problem of achieving efficiency in a narrower sense— the problem of allocating resources so as to yield the appropriate mix of outputs other than liberty. I shall give brief attention to this matter of consumers' freedom, and the line of demarcation is not easy to draw; but this kind of freedom will not be my chief concern. Even choosing among job opportunities will be considered as an aspect of consumers' sovereignty, though a moderate restriction of choice here would be more damaging to most persons than a moderate restriction of choice between "clothing and automobile opportunities." Pushed far enough, of course, either type of restriction can make people very unhappy.

impacts on consumers' sovereignty

In most societies, past or present, government spending has involved large reductions of freedom in the sense of providing services that many individual taxpayers would not voluntarily buy. Taxes are compulsory, and we have no way of knowing just how each individual would choose to use the resources if they were left in his hands; but we know that pacifists would not buy defense, childless couples would hardly spend as much as they now do on the education of other people's children, and people near Seattle would not contribute as heavily as at present toward the purchase of irrigation in Arizona.

Many government services have public-good characteristics, and it is uneconomical to charge admission and find out what consumers would voluntarily choose. As mentioned earlier, defense and flood control are examples. If these goods are to be provided at all, it is probably sensible to use compulsory assessments or taxes. In other cases, even though the government services could be sold and consumers' freedom of choice could be maintained, government uses compulsory taxes anyway and impairs this freedom. Thus for one reason or another government spending does not cater to individuals' choices in old-age insurance, education, defense, foreign aid, research and development, and so on.

Similarly, minority-group choices are often neglected. When governments tax and spend, they do things that the group in power wishes, and in democracies these things approximate what majority coalitions want. Government taxing and spending policies, then, often impair the freedom of choice of minority groups—American Indians, perhaps, or groups that would like to have religion taught in the schools, or those women who are forced to pay Social Security taxes even though they will not work long enough to be eligible for Social Security benefits. The point is the same as before: government taxation and spending reduces the ability of minority groups to buy what they prefer just as it reduces the ability of individual taxpayers to do so. That is, it impairs minority sovereignty just as it impairs consumer sovereignty.

In addition to imposing taxes, which are directly linked with public outlays, governments restrict consumers' choices in ways that are not closely related to the volume of spending. Consumers cannot buy certain medicines without prescriptions, purchase the services of unlicensed barbers, or buy tickets to New York via San Francisco from an intra-California carrier. They cannot buy or own an eagle (according to Federal law). A few decades ago the consumer was not supposed to buy liquor. Today he may be forbidden to buy an automobile that is not equipped with a prescribed smog-control device, even if he lives in the High Sierras. If one combed our national, state and local statutes and ordinances, one could compile a tremendous list of forbidden items. And in many other countries such lists are much longer.

The reduction of choice, and any other ill effects, must be weighed against the desirable effects of these activities when each of us decides whether to support or oppose public expenditures. One thing that should be kept in mind is that, strictly speaking, consumers' sovereignty is bound to be violated to some extent in any event because of externalities and because of the interdependence among utility functions. Voluntary exchange and individual consumers' choices, as ordinarily defined, would not completely avoid coercion of other consumers either, because if Brown sells my neighbor Jones a Rolls-Royce (a voluntary exchange that makes both of *them* better off), it may thrust upon me a loss of satisfaction because of my envy of Jones.[3] This may not be as long-lived or as significant a deprivation of my freedom of choice as that represented by my annual tax bill, but such things are hard to compare.

Perhaps it should also be emphasized that innovation and economic growth have, over the last few decades, greatly increased the range of individual choice for most people. As a consequence, it may be that now the marginal loss of free choice caused by public taxation and spending is not very great. Moreover, some government programs, such as those for education, research and development, the extension of opportunity, the increase of mobility, and the prevention of deflation, may stimulate innovation and production and thereby expand the range of choice among goods for all of us. (Other programs may of course promote instability or discourage innovation and prosperity.) Finally, it is clear that subsidies and transfer payments increase the range of choice open to particular groups while decreasing the range of consumers' choice open to others. Thus these impacts on freedom of choice are not all one way. In any event, while the effect of government spending on consumers' and minorities' sovereignty should be noted, I shall consider this as an effect on other aspects of well-being, not as a *direct* impact on the basic freedoms. As will be noted later, however, the restriction of consumers' and employees' options may have significant *indirect* effects on these other freedoms, because these kinds of freedoms or options are to some extent substitutes, and if the cost of one kind goes up, or if it becomes relatively scarce, the price of the other tends to go up also.

other constraints on individuals

Government places many other kinds of constraints on individuals. It may prohibit farmers from planting certain crops on certain acreages. It may prohibit growers from marketing grapefruit of less than a designated size or prohibit employers from hiring laborers for less than a designated wage. The choices of a home-builder or contractor are limited by building codes. Instead of making a flat prohibition or requirement, government often simply penalizes undesired behavior. If the farmer departs from his quota, he sacrifices the opportunity to sell at the support price. If the owner of a building fails to meet

---

[3] Bator, *op. cit.*, pp. 86–87.

prescribed standards, he is fined. In most instances like these the government acts because of pressure from some producer organization or other group; but then *all* government action is the result of pressure from one influential group or another, for example, the majority of voters.

Government contractors face many specific constraints—limitations on personnel policies, requirements that reports and forms be submitted on specified dates, and rules about specific decisions. Signing contracts within the private sector confronts the signers with constraints, of course; but governmental bodies and administrators are almost inevitably led, by the cost-reward structures they face, to introduce a relatively large number of specific requirements. Recipients of welfare or other transfer payments must conform to certain conditions or sacrifice the money. The American tourist may travel and make purchases abroad, but he must pay a penalty if he brings many purchases home with him.

In addition to the requirements they would face in the private sector, government employees must usually satisfy other stated requirements and observe certain rules in order to obtain and retain their positions. No matter how good a teacher is, he must meet certain formal requirements, which vary from state to state, before he is given a teaching certificate. For many positions a person must have lived the "right" kind of life to obtain a security clearance and be eligible for employment. Government regulations make it necessary for lawyers, accountants, and many others to be certified even for private employment.

These interferences have some good effects and some bad ones. Restrictions on entry into occupations exist in part because some group wants shelter from competition. But licenses and certificates and required labels are also a way of providing information: they tell one that the probability is relatively high that a member of the set of persons having this certificate or label has certain capabilities. (This may or may not be an economical way of providing that information.) In most instances, then, there are gains to be weighed against the costs. Moreover, while these interferences generally increase with increased government spending, there is not necessarily a high correlation. Restrictions of this sort can be imposed and enforced with comparatively little government spending, and it would be possible to have large expenditures without having many of these constraints.

In some governments these various restrictions have become so numerous and pervasive that they have constituted an obvious and serious impairment of freedom. In the United States they may not have seriously reduced freedom of choice; there are still numerous options. Here I shall look upon them much as I viewed the impairments of consumers' sovereignty (to which they are closely related)—I shall view them as having effects on economic efficiency but as being minor *direct* limitations on freedom.

factors that make it expensive to exercise or guard one's basic rights

Let us turn to the fundamental freedoms that are enumerated in the Bill of Rights and ask what utility maximization can tell us, if anything, about the conditions under which they are likely to be eroded. As we noted in earlier chapters, our analytical tool, the basic tool of economic theory, is a simple one. It is merely the theorem that demand curves for all things are negatively inclined: If something becomes relatively expensive, individuals will take less of it, and if something becomes relatively inexpensive, they will take more of it. This basic proposition has been rather thoroughly tested and appears to be correct. The possible implications discussed in this study, however, are highly speculative, because I may be wrong in believing that more government spending, or more centralization, makes the indicated forms of behavior relatively expensive. One force may work to make those forms of behavior relatively expensive, but other things may not remain constant. Perhaps some other force that I leave out of account works simultaneously to make those forms of behavior relatively inexpensive. If part of the orange crop is ruined, but technological advances simultaneously increase productivity in orange production, the cost of oranges to consumers may go down instead of up. Thus, while in my view this framework is a useful one by means of which to seek the implications of various institutional arrangements, it must be used with care—like any other partial-equilibrium analysis.

To maintain one's rights is costly. At best it is disturbingly expensive to guard or "purchase" one's freedoms or to stand up for the rights of individuals in general. There is the now-familiar point that, from the standpoint of each individual, voting and especially acquiring information about candidates and issues ordinarily involve costs like time and energy yet offer infinitesimal probabilities of affecting elections and therefore small expected rewards. Similar considerations apply to protesting any impairment of one's rights or of other individuals' rights. First, consider an infringement of someone else's rights. If some stranger is denied his right to vote, most persons decide that even the relatively modest effort of sending letters to their senators takes time and offers virtually no reward. If the FCC threatens a left-wing or right-wing radio station, or refuses to renew the license of one, those with relatively high stakes and those whose rights are directly threatened will complain, but few "outsiders" are likely to spend money or time protesting. The reason: one individual's action would ordinarily have little impact on (1) that particular incident or (2) the probability that those outsiders will suffer subsequent infringements of their rights.

To be sure, one can cite instances in which outsiders do enter the lists. Some do incur the high cost of forming or supporting organizations to protect individual liberties. Many persons other than those whose rights have been denied have taken up the cause of civil rights, particularly the protection of the Negro's right to vote. Sometimes this involvement is the result of a combination of events that arouses strong emotions, which then makes action have a payoff to the actor. When emotions run high, unfortunately, another high cost enters the picture. The persons concerned often lose sight of the goal of protecting all individuals' rights and become perfectly willing to sacrifice the rights of some persons to further particular objectives. If this goes far enough, it may make it still more difficult to protect the basic freedoms. At other times the action of bystanders may be prompted by a considered concern for individual rights, either for idealistic reasons or for fear that infringements may spread and affect the bystanders themselves. Nonetheless, except in rather special circumstances, individual bystanders do not find it sufficiently rewarding to intervene when someone else's rights are threatened.[4] Such behavior is not surprising or necessarily reprehensible. As the individual scans his T-account, it appears to be costly and comparatively unrewarding to act. Most of the rewards are external: decreases in the probability that *other* people's rights will be eroded. To individuals in the aggregate the reward from action, the chance of effecting a favorable outcome times the aggregate value of a favorable outcome, is large, but in such situations it is also very costly to individuals to organize group action.[5] (For these same reasons, one seldom finds consumers voicing strenuous objections to a tariff.) As a consequence, the maintenance of individual rights is at best a difficult matter, and the price of freedom is indeed high.

Consider next one's reaction to the erosion of his own rights. Even in this case one often finds it relatively costly and unrewarding to take a firm stand. Suppose my name was mysteriously deleted from the list of registered voters. Fretting about it might not be worth much perspiration. Suppose I was taken from my home in the middle of the night and put in jail for a few days without being charged. How *much* time and money would I later spend to protest? Suppose I would lose a valued contract if I criticized the administration. Would I voice the criticism? The answers to such questions depend upon several things —the values I attach to various rights, my assessment of the impact of these events on the probability of losing those rights, my assessment of the chances that my action would have any effect on future events, the values I attach to alternative uses of my time, and so on. Different people will behave in different

---

[4] Indeed, as has been stressed in the newspapers, bystanders frequently fail to intervene to protect someone else's life.

[5] Mancur Olson, Jr., *The Logic of Collective Action*, Harvard University Press, Cambridge, Mass., 1965, especially pp. 53–97.

ways, but one thing is clear: It is expensive to stand up for one's own rights, let alone the rights of others.

A reduction in the range of options makes it more costly to protect one's rights. If a person has relatively few attractive options, such as alternative employers, it becomes still more expensive to him to protect his rights or those of others.[6] If, on the one hand, I can turn to alternative jobs without great sacrifice, it does not cost me much to stand up to my present employer or supervisor or colleague or client—to refuse to allow anyone to tell me what to write or say, or to tolerate discrimination against me because of my race or religion. If, on the other hand, there are only a few options of value open, it is more important for me to hold on to my present employment and not to foreclose any of my comparatively few opportunities. In other words it is more important for me to get along with employers, colleagues, and so on; I am more dependent on their opinions of me. To write or speak or worship in ways that displease them is more expensive to me than it would be if I had a better range of options. I am likely to take less of these items because their prices are higher; that is, I am more likely to speak cautiously and perhaps endure direct impairments of my freedom than I would be if I had a wide range of options. Options other than employment are pertinent too. If there are few alternatives regarding my children's schools, an apartment or house, ration coupons, recreation facilities, or permission to start a business or borrow funds, my dependence upon some persons' favors increases. I may accept more limitations on my liberty because the price of exercising my freedom has gone up. One of the most important means of keeping that price down is having the ability to vote with my feet, that is, having a diversity of stores or schools or banks or communities to which I can turn. In this indirect way consumers' choices in general are important to the basic freedoms, because they are to some extent substitutes.

As will be stressed again later, the "quantity" of freedom produced for each individual depends not only on this variable, the effect of options on the cost of standing up for one's rights, but also on other variables, such as the tastes and traditions of the citizenry, the values and beliefs of officials and men of influence, the legal framework, and the extent of checks and balances. All that is being suggested here is that, other things remaining the same, fewer options can make the exercise of the basic freedoms more expensive to individuals.

---

[6] Many of the points made in this chapter have often been made, employing somewhat different terminology, with respect to the broad extremes—socialism versus capitalism. One of the clearest presentations is Milton Friedman, *Capitalism and Freedom*, The University of Chicago Press, Chicago, 1962, pp. 1–21. To a considerable extent I have simply tried to convert such thoughts about the costs or difficulties of maintaining freedom into a continuous rather than a "two-case" cost function.

Special favors can make it more costly to preserve one's rights. Not only the loss of valuable options but also the creation of special favors, bribes, or threats can increase the cost of exercising or guarding one's freedom. If speaking or worshiping freely entails the sacrifice of large rewards or the threat of severe punishments, the exercise of these freedoms is costly. If someone offers me an especially highpaying job to keep my mouth shut or to keep left- or right-wing programs off the air, it becomes relatively expensive for me to preserve my liberties or to worry about those of others. To take an extreme case, the Nazis made it highly rewarding to forget about individual rights and almost prohibitively costly to be concerned about them.

Effects of government spending on these factors. What connection does government spending have with these factors? Public spending and government activities can, up to a point and in certain ways, increase the range of options open to most individuals. For example, certain types of spending for court systems, law enforcement, education, health, job training, employment exchanges, dissemination of information, and mobility allowances may expand the range of choices for most persons, thus reducing the cost to them of exercising their independence. Some government activities expand the range of options open to particular groups, thus decreasing the cost of those persons maintaining their freedoms. Programs to offer better training to Negroes, and to reduce the barriers facing them, make it less difficult for them to acquire or protect their basic freedoms. (On the other hand, constraints like the minimum-wage law reduce the options open to the "disadvantaged," who must then engage in a desperate search for ways to employ themselves at less than the legal minimum.) It seems highly appropriate to assist such groups, even though it implies reducing the range of choice facing others, in order to make the costs of protecting individual rights more nearly equal. Appropriate monetary-fiscal policy, although not necessarily correlated with the volume of public spending, is another activity that, by preventing deflation, can increase the number of job options confronting individuals. On balance, I would certainly argue that many public activities help widen the range of choices open to most people and equalize the cost of guarding their basic rights.

Beyond some point, however, government spending can begin to reduce options. At the extreme, if government were the only employer and were comparatively monolithic, I would have few job choices and would express myself rather cautiously. Even with the high levels of public spending that exist today, of course, most persons in the United States have numerous job options—multiple Federal employers, state agencies, municipal governments, semi-independent agencies, and, far more numerous, private firms. By incurring costs, one can usually send his child to the public school in his district, to a different public school, or to a private school; or, though it may entail a high cost, one can move to a different community (though clearly for some groups the options are severely limited). For services one can turn to alternative stores, banks, or apartment owners. With many options open, a person is not likely to feel unusual pressure to neglect or surrender his freedoms. Nonetheless, large additions to government spending could enlarge the role of government as an employer and a provider of services and thereby gradually raise the cost of being concerned about one's freedoms.

Obviously the effect of increased government spending depends upon many variables, such as the degree of autonomy of local governments, the separation of powers within governmental units, the degree of decentralization within government, the traditions or rules that constrain governmental authorities, and the *types* of tax and expenditure programs. If government confined its activities to the provision of *general* benefits that could not be withheld from particular groups, the spending would give relatively little leverage to anyone. If the rules were always unambiguous, even to legislative bodies, for awarding contracts or welfare payments or tax shelter, no branch of government would have much discretionary power that might induce individuals to sacrifice basic rights. Programs and institutions can certainly be designed so as to reduce (or increase) the risks.

For almost any *given* set of rules, however, greatly increased public outlays are likely to bring at least slightly higher risks—somewhat higher costs to many individuals of maintaining their basic rights. Government activities always involve hiring and firing individuals, not generalized humanity; tax and disbursement provisions differ for different groups and individuals. In real life, neither benefits nor taxes are completely general, information is not costless, and rules cannot be clear-cut. When the Sierra Club opposed the government's proposed dams in the Grand Canyon, officials *did* have a way of making this opposition expensive—namely, through the Internal Revenue Service's threat to withdraw the tax shelter previously enjoyed by the organization. Eventually various recipients of benefits might think twice about criticizing whatever coalition was in power, because the defeat of that coalition at the polls might divert benefits to other groups. It is said that in certain Communist nations patronage rather than overt coercion is now the major instrument of control—that, if one speaks too freely, he risks having his police card stamped "politically undesirable," which makes it difficult to get a car license, a good job or apartment, a passport, and so on. A large purse *can* mean power; and compared with governments, even giant corporations have small purses and little authority. A $500 billion U.S. budget might make it quite expensive to maintain checks and balances in government and the basic rights of citizens.

There is another way in which increased government spending may bring about fewer attractive options and make concern about liberties more expensive to individuals. If the government becomes a relatively large property owner or absorbs property rights by imposing heavy taxes or numerous constraints on property owners, the result may be a reduction in the range of job choices and other options open to people. The dispersal of property rights among individuals produces a multiplicity of options, giving more choices to households (with private as well as public schools to choose among), more options of setting up independent enterprises of one's own (a special sort of job option), more options of working for others who set up independent enterprises, and more ways of trading wealth for job and other options. The heavier the tax on income from properties, the less rewarding it is to set up enterprises; and if there are sufficient constraints on the use of properties, it may be costly to offer or to seek options. The fewer ways there are to trade wealth for options, the more costly it is to be a "non-preferred person"[7] (e.g., an old, colored, handicapped, inexperienced, left-wing, right-wing, or ugly person). If carried far enough, this could be a serious matter.

Another way in which the growth of government spending, particularly at the Federal level, could reduce options is by stimulating government centralization. As stressed in Chapter 10, when firms or local governments behave in ways that one dislikes, one can as a last resort vote with his feet. The fewer the levels of independent governments, the less the degree of competition among government units, and the more monolithic the structure and the fewer the bargaining influences, the less recourse one has when faced with arbitrary decisions.

It might be noted that reductions in options and increases in the cost of freedoms probably make it easier for further steps in that direction to occur. Taking one step does not force one to go all the way; having some government intervention and trying to prevent further intervention is not like jumping off the Empire State Building and trying to stop. But the production of power concentration may well be a decreasing-cost industry. If people find their options restricted and the exercise of their basic freedom more costly than before, they are likely to protest less; and this may in turn make it less expensive to officials to reduce options further (see the next section). As voters receive certain favors, for example, it becomes more expensive to vote in such a way as to eliminate those favors. Tacit agreement can play a larger role than overt compulsion, especially in the early stages of power concentration. If enough variables work in the same direction, it is easy to see how a Nazi Germany can

---

[7] Harold Demsetz, "Minorities in the Marketplace," *North Carolina Law Review*, February, 1965, pp. 271–297.

evolve. Perhaps the remarkable thing is not that it has happened but that it doesn't happen even more often.

factors that make it inexpensive to interfere with individuals' rights

The factors discussed so far have been those that make it more or less difficult for a person to exercise his so-called basic rights. Let us now turn to the other side of the coin—to the factors that make it more or less difficult for one person to interfere with others' basic rights. In what circumstances can someone begin to throw his weight around without sacrificing much? In part, I have already answered this question: If one can influence the direction of government expenditures, award jobs or favors to persons who have few options, or offer particularly attractive rewards or options or threats, one will find it somewhat easier than it would otherwise be to interfere with someone's basic rights. There is little point, however, in reviewing these factors merely from a different vantage point. It may be more useful to examine the roles of two particular factors —property rights and voting rights.

Dilution of individual property rights. One circumstance that may give some persons the ability to throw their weight around is the extensive attenuation of *individual* property rights. A strong tradition of maintaining such rights makes it relatively costly for persons with a reason or taste for oppression to indulge. This is because property rights give persons a base, so to speak, from which to strike back at would-be oppressors. This is true even for people who do not own property, as long as a diversity of other individuals does. Individual property rights imply that people cannot do as they please with or on someone else's property. Thus, government or corporation officials can properly regulate my speech or other activities on *their* properties—but they cannot regulate my speech or worship on properties that *I* rent or buy (as long as I do not disturb the peace or break other laws). If they try to regulate my activities on my own property, there are fairly clear-cut steps by means of which I can sue and impose costs on them. These steps are not prohibitively expensive, and individual or small-group action has a good chance of being effective. Moreover, other persons, seeing their rights threatened, can also take similar steps to impose costs on the potential oppressor. Thus, individual property rights, if they are at least somewhat dispersed, can make extreme selfishness expensive. That is, it can make it expensive to disregard the damages one inflicts on others or to interfere with their right to speak, publish, worship, or assemble. (If only a few persons hold all the property, of course, or if the distribution of wealth is so unequal that minorities cannot possibly rent properties for their purposes, or if the wealthy can employ government to restrict entry and exchange, these cost functions will be somewhat different.)

Without individual property rights, with all properties owned by government, officials would have to decide what activities were legitimate. (It is nonsense to think that publicly owned properties would somehow become free goods.) Officials might reach decisions that infringed on people's freedoms. Through the courts people could still try to impose costs on officials who impaired their basic rights. But the rules, and the criteria of infringement, would be less clear-cut, and the cost of the information needed for a court decision would be greater. And the courts might have *even greater* difficulty in maintaining objectivity. Organizing political pressures rather than using court procedures, on the other hand, would be relatively costly to an individual or minority group and have less chance of success. If all this is correct, officials might in this milieu find it less costly to them to engage in oppressive acts.

To be sure, such factors could be counteracted by strong traditions, skill in maintaining checks and balances, heroic efforts on the part of certain groups, and so on. The outcome depends upon numerous variables, and it is certainly not being suggested that oppression will inevitably follow if individual property rights are somewhat attenuated or if public spending doubles. In Great Britain public spending is large, and the scope of individual property rights has been reduced, yet I see no evidence that the freedoms of speech, worship, or press are threatened. In some Eastern Socialist countries, although government activity is extensive and individual property rights have been greatly restricted, citizens seem to speak freely in private (but they do not seem to have *effective* freedom of press, worship, assembly, voting, or public speech). To repeat: Big spending and the dilution of individual property rights, if pushed far enough, make it more difficult, though not necessarily impossible, to maintain the basic freedoms.

Nor is it being suggested that oppression can always be avoided if public spending is modest and individual property rights are unrestricted. In *any* economic system there will be some infringement of individual rights. (As the old saying goes: Under capitalism man oppresses man, while under socialism it is just the reverse.) All that one can realistically hope to do is to identify some of the trade-offs that can help one seek the less imperfect arrangements.

Suppose, as illustrations, that officials decided to eliminate the Pacifica Foundation, to forbid meetings of the Birch Society, to raze the house of a Negro in a white neighborhood to provide room for a small park, to ban speeches opposing U.S. defense efforts in Southeast Asia, or to forbid the advocacy of military efforts in Southeast Asia. Without a tradition of individual property rights, how could people object? Not by the *relatively* inexpensive means of lawsuits referring to their rights to use *their* properties for their own purposes. They would have to turn to comparatively difficult routes—to lawsuits contending that they had rights to use specific public properties for these purposes or to expensive attempts to sway public opinion and organize political pressures. There is nothing sacrosanct or God-given about individual property rights—but a considerable reliance on them may be an economical arrangement for making oppression of individuals or minorities expensive to oppressors. And the fact that individual property rights do not always ensure the preservation of other rights does not mean that government property rights would automatically be better.

Another important factor that makes control relatively costly to the oppressor is vigorous competition among independent enterprises. In a highly competitive industry, it is expensive for management to devote resources to purchasing nonpecuniary benefits[8]—to emphasizing beauty more than competence when hiring secretaries, printing pamphlets supporting antivivisection, indulging in a preference for racial discrimination,[9] indulging in a taste for right- or left-wing views, or pressuring employees to vote in a particular way. If competition is keen, the penalty for pursuing such nonpecuniary goals is bankruptcy. If competition is less vigorous, there is more room for the purchase of nonpecuniary emoluments,[10] but even moderate competition—even rivalry among independent not-for-profit institutions or governmental units—makes it more expensive than it would otherwise be for officials to trade performance for concern about an employee's race, creed, color, manner of voting, personal life, political views, and so on. Thus, in the terminology used in the preceding section, competition makes it comparatively expensive for officials to create special options that may induce one to abandon the exercise of his rights.

For this reason, too, the dilution of individual property rights may make the abridgment of freedom less difficult for men of influence. Heavy taxation of business profits works in this direction, making it less costly to managers of firms to purchase nonpecuniary gains (that is, they sacrifice less when they purchase such benefits). Extensive use of not-for-profit corporations and government enterprises dilutes individual property rights. Also, the less the rivalry among independent units, the more nonpecuniary benefits officials in not-for-profit corporations and government enterprises can afford to buy. In not-for-

---

[8] Armen A. Alchian and Reuben Kessel, "Competition, Monopoly, and the Pursuit of Money," *Aspects of Labor Economics*, A Report of the National Bureau of Economic Research, Princeton University Press, Princeton, N.J., 1962, pp. 157–183.

[9] Unless *most* customers have a strong taste for goods and services produced by "preferred" persons. See Gary S. Becker, *The Economics of Discrimination*, The University of Chicago Press, Chicago, 1957; and Demsetz, "Minorities in the Marketplace."

[10] Oliver E. Williamson, *The Economics of Discretionary Behavior*, Prentice-Hall, Inc., Englewood Cliffs, N.J., 1964.

profit and government undertakings, complicated constraints are imposed on management to prevent the purchase of certain nonpecuniary satisfactions, but for the sake of preserving some flexibility a good deal of discretion usually remains, including some discretion to discriminate among employees. Indeed, as Demsetz has pointed out, many governmental interferences with free markets—minimum-wage laws, equal-pay laws, support of union power, price ceilings—prevent "nonpreferred" persons from offering compensation to offset the wish to discriminate. The result is to reduce the number of options open to "nonpreferred" persons and add further to the disadvantage of such minorities.[11] One of the consequences can be to raise the cost to minorities of exercising their basic rights and lower the cost to decision makers of encroaching on these individuals' freedoms. Businessmen and officials may find it a little less costly to interfere with individuals' rights directly or to create special rewards and penalties to induce them to abandon the exercise of their rights.

This is merely to point out certain disadvantageous implications of diluting private property rights. It does not indicate that no such actions should be taken. Government programs, which require taxation and some dilution of individual property rights, bring gains as well as disadvantages. Having not-for-profit corporations and government agencies is often better than any known alternative. And, while rivalry among independent units may reduce the likelihood that our basic freedoms will be eroded, an infinite number of autonomous units would cost more than it would be worth. To repeat, I am merely focusing attention on part of the relevant considerations—ones that may, however, be relatively neglected.

What does all this discussion have to do with public spending? *Beyond some level,* public spending with its accompanying taxation and constraints (1) dilutes individual property rights, and (2) reduces the degree of competition among independent enterprises. If the preceding argument is correct, these impacts can make it less expensive to men of influence to interfere with other persons' basic freedoms. Up to a fairly heavy volume of government spending and in favorable circumstances, the effects may be trivial. With further expansion of public activities, however, these effects may become cumulatively more significant. Bigger government and increased centralization may be like growing older; at any particular moment it seems a bit foolish to be alarmed about it, yet ultimately it can be fatal.

Lack of effective voting rights. It presumably needs little emphasis, but a tremendously important factor in preserving other individual freedoms is the maintenance of individual voting rights. If one has a vote that is genuinely

---

[11] Demsetz, *op. cit.*

valuable to politicians and thence to officials, they will pay a price for it, and the price can include a considerable respect for basic rights. If officialdom violates the rights of individuals having such votes, the individuals can make the violations costly to officials. If an individual or set of individuals has no effective vote, however, it becomes less expensive for officials or others to interfere with those individuals' freedoms.

The effects are fairly obvious in the case of Negroes in parts of the United States where they have often had no vote at all. Since elected officials have not depended on the Negroes' votes, they have provided them with relatively poor street repairs, schools, sanitation, and public services. Perhaps more importantly, officials can dispense harsher punishments, permit inferior jury trials, and prevent Negroes from speaking freely—without paying much of a penalty. At least some difference in these respects is said to exist in cities where Negroes have begun voting. The effects are also plain to see in authoritarian societies, where citizens get to vote, but only for one set of candidates. Again, no one depends upon anyone's vote, no one is willing to trade anything for it, and officials can disregard individual rights without much cost to themselves. Settling matters by majority vote may not be highly satisfactory, but democratic government has much to commend it in comparison with the alternatives. In particular, possession of votes that politicians value is essential to the preservation of individual rights.

Voting rights are, of course, an "intermediate" safeguard that depend themselves upon something else—upon some sort of consensus or agreement to live according to a set of rules. Or, perhaps voting rights are a necessary but not a sufficient condition for the maintenance of individual liberty. Another necessary condition may be an agreement to disperse power *in an operational fashion* by maintaining fairly extensive *individual* property rights. Given their other attributes and arrangements for voluntary exchange, some such property system is probably the lowest-cost way to preserve (with some designated probability) other individual rights. In the long run, a system of this sort may be especially valuable to conspicuous minorities. Such systems do not insure everyone's freedom or eliminate injustice and evil—but the relevant question is not "Is anything wrong with a particular arrangement?" but rather "What changes seem likely to offer improvements?"

does the unseen hand lead to ever-larger public outlays?

Does utility maximization by voters, political parties, politicians, and officials imply ever-larger government and, if the above arguments are correct, ultimately a lower likelihood of maintaining individual rights? There is no clear-cut answer, for there are forces working in both directions. In general it may seem that spending proposals are more likely to succeed than proposals to cut spending. On the one hand, officials, politicians, and citizens who benefit from government expenditures frequently benefit considerably—enough to make active support worth its cost to those individuals. On the other hand, the ill effects are often spread over a larger group (voters who pay taxes but receive no benefits, politicians whose constituents pay taxes but receive no benefits, officials who compete for their slices of the budget), and the damages felt per individual may be slight—not enough to make active opposition worth the cost.[12] For proposals to cut spending, the lineup of forces tends to be just the opposite.

Another force that may lead to larger government spending, one that was noted earlier, is the fact that power acquisition may be a decreasing-cost output. Larger government spending may make successively larger increments of power easier to obtain. Thus for several reasons one might conclude that there are built-in tendencies for public spending to increase.

But there are clearly pressures to restrain government spending also. People recognize considerations over and above the direct effects of each proposal. The fact that public outlays do not expand so as to include the entire national income indicates that restraining forces exist. Private consumption demands mean that beyond some point a majority would object violently to even small increases in taxes per capita. Majorities of voters in a jurisdictional unit are often unwilling, when distribution of the costs and gains are fairly clear, to provide services for minorities, unless they value the minorities' support greatly on other matters. (Older sections of a city do not like to finance facilities for annexed suburbs.) Decisions about the scale of public outlays depend upon the combination of issues that confront politicians and voters and upon the resulting bargaining network—but it is plain to see that there are constraining forces and that in the right circumstances they could even lead to cuts in public activities. Vague fears of governmental authority, which once constituted an effective restraint, may still linger. In any event there are many crosscurrents, and there is nothing predetermined about where the unseen hand will lead us regarding the volume of public spending and regarding the extent of individual liberty. We can choose—we can make use of the unseen hand rather than let it make use of us.

---

[12] See James M. Buchanan and Gordon Tullock, *The Calculus of Consent*, University of Michigan Press, Ann Arbor, Mich., 1962, pp. 164–169.

part
three

SOME TOOLS FOR SHAPING PUBLIC CHOICES

eight

As has been stressed repeatedly, there is no definite criterion of correct public spending policies. People can disagree, without departing from the principles of logic, about to what extent whose wishes should be satisfied. Fortunately, economic analysis can nevertheless help us in evaluating public spending policies, particularly if we keep in mind the basic limitations noted. Tools do not have to be perfect in order to be helpful.

The tool to be considered here comprises calculations of costs and/or benefits of alternative policies to help decision makers reach better choices. A budget is usually an estimate of costs alone, and a "cost-benefit" analysis includes estimates of both. Either sort of calculation may be called an "economic calculus." It can never point indisputably to *the* right choice, from the standpoint of either an individual or a group. For there is no group utility function, and the choice of each individual depends upon his own values. (As for Pareto optimality, it is extremely difficult in the absence of markets to obtain information about individual evaluations of various costs and benefits.) Furthermore, the physical and sociological consequences of alternative policies cannot be predicted with certainty, and in the end each person has to make a personal judgment as to the probability of various consequences.

How then can calculations and analytical aids be useful? There are at least two ways in which most economists believe they can help. First, they can provide information, after the fashion of consumers' research, that often appears to be worth its cost. How can one tell whether economic analysis or consumers' research is worth its cost? In the private sphere, the only test is survival in the market. In the public sphere the only test is one's judgment or perhaps survival in the political process. Like consumers' research, an economic calculus pertaining to public policies may provide information that is only slightly relevant to the decisions of a few persons or that is highly relevant to the choices and views of many persons. In designing analytical aids, one tries, of course, to steer toward information that is relatively useful.

Calculations or analysis pertaining to government proposals can often be applied to choices in connection with which most people do agree on certain values, at least in the sense of agreeing to accept the results of a certain decision-making process. Then that process may lead to a decision to carry out a specified task, such as providing more water, or improving the allocation of water, in a particular region. Many individual voters implicitly decide that this task is of greater value than alternative tasks. They may also implicitly condone the use of observed prices (or in some instances imputed prices) as value tags in tracing out the costs and benefits of alternative ways of carrying out the task. In other words, on certain issues there may in effect exist a working agreement regarding some of the relevant preferences. If analyses are linked with some of the values of government officials, they should also be linked with certain values held by numerous individual citizens. (If this is not so, only a change in the bargaining framework can help; altering the analyses will not lead to decisions widely approved by citizens.)

There need be nothing illogical about dissenting or disregarding analytical aids, and one should not lose sight of the fact that value judgments are being made. The calculations will reveal nothing about many of the impacts on individual utility functions (see Chapters 4 and 5). But the estimates usually have a bearing on "economic efficiency," which *may* emerge from the bargaining process as *one* of the major, agreed-upon values.

Moreover, the alternatives may be ones for which the positive sciences can trace out the principal physical and behavioral consequences with a high degree of confidence. In analyzing a region's water-supply problems, physical scientists may be able to predict quite accurately what would happen if alternative desalinization plants were constructed, if water was conveyed to the fields by alternative pumping systems and subsurface aquifers, if the water was applied to various acreages in various quantities. Economists may be able to say how individuals would respond to alternative price structures and the consequent agricultural development of the region. Sociologists may be able to predict the effects, perhaps trivial in this instance, of the relocation of families and industries on crime, mental health, and juvenile delinquency. Needless to say, these and other predictions would not be completely accurate. Dissent on the basis of one's personal judgments about these things need not be illogical, since the positive sciences still contain many gaps. But again, for some sets of alternatives, most persons' judgments may be similar. Hence, analyses may be valuable because they can help numerous individuals identify choices that they prefer.

A second way in which an economic calculus can help is by causing officials and citizens to look at problems of choice in the right way, even if all the quantities and values have to be filled in on the basis of judgment. The estimation of costs and benefits, or even costs alone, as in budgets, virtually cries out for the examination of alternatives instead of the attempt to identify unique needs. In other words, the analytical aids that will be discussed here may at least help one to raise the right questions. It is hard to believe that one can make good decisions by asking the wrong questions.

conventional budgeting

One aid that can work toward raising the right questions and providing relevant information is improved budgeting exhibits. Current budget formats and decision-making procedures vary a great deal within the Federal government and among state and local governments. In recent decades there has been much experimentation, and many improvements have been effected. It is almost certain, however, that further significant improvements can be made.

Often the budget categories that officials must consider increasing or decreasing (for example, general government; commerce, housing, and space technology; labor and welfare) are too broad for good judgments to be made about their relative size. Sometimes the categories are account titles or organization units, such as the Public Health Service or the Bureau of Land Management, that include conglomerations of activities more closely related to the work of other agencies than to each other. Often the categories are across-the-board inputs, such as "salaries and expenses," "travel," or "printing," that help produce a variety of outputs but are not linked in a discernible way with any particular output.

Furthermore, the existing process of budget formulation is frequently one in which physical "requirements" are selected prior to cost estimation. Thus many choices are made without conscious reference to costs, that is, to the alternative benefits that must be sacrificed. To be sure, some kind of cost constraints are recognized, since the lists of "requirements" or "needs" are not infinitely long. In addition, explicit budget constraints are introduced in later stages of budget formulation. Thus an iterative process occurs in which both needs and costs are considered. The "need-firsters" (those who try to figure out what is needed regardless of cost) compromise concerning "indispensable requirements," and the "budget-firsters" (those who try to perceive how much can be spent regardless of benefit) compromise concerning "absolute budget ceilings." Nonetheless, many choices become imbedded in the budget at an early stage, and other choices are made under pressure at later stages, without conscious or careful comparison of benefits with costs.

These effects can be described in terms of neglected interdependencies. When officials reach decisions about such expenditure categories and by means of the procedures just described, it is extremely difficult for them to take crucial interrelationships into account and therefore to make reasonable judgments about the costs and gains from alternative outlays. Many persons become disturbed by the neglect of a kind of interdependency called "duplication." The value of the missile Thor depended upon whether or not another agency was developing Jupiter, and the value of reclaiming arid acreages depends upon whether or not another agency is reclaiming swampy lands; yet the budgeting process often does not seem to take such interrelationships into account.

As noted before, another critical interrelationship that received scant attention was the relationship between the need for one thing and the need for other things, that is, between benefit and cost. The desirability of having one government service depends upon what alternative services would have to be sacrificed to provide it. Yet this is overlooked—trade-offs are neglected—if requirements are drawn up with little reference to costs.

Focusing attention on input categories also leads to the neglect of the connection between the inputs and the functions or purposes of the various activities. How many people or typewriters to employ certainly depends upon what functions are to be performed. A budget in terms of typewriters, personnel, and travel (added together for various functions) makes it difficult to relate these ingredients to the desired outputs and therefore to make sound judgments about the amounts to buy. Although the lower-level programming process no doubt relates the inputs to tasks to be performed, bulky exhibits of across-the-board inputs give little help to higher-level officials in making judgments about the proposed purchases. Similarly, if a bakery manager tried to decide how much flour, sugar, and butter to buy without linking these items to the amounts of bread and pastries to be produced, he would be handicapped in reaching good decisions.

Another difficulty with existing budget formats is that they usually show the costs (proposed expenditures or obligational authority) for only one year in advance. In the case of many choices, one-year costs represent only the down payment and fail to indicate substantial future costs implied by the proposed activities. These future costs are not always inevitable, once the activity has been started, for they may still be avoided by cancellation of the activity. Nonetheless, the future costs are often implied, because once a substantial investment has been made, it will probably be economical to complete the program and incur the additional costs. The probable full costs, not just the down payment, should be recognized at the outset, just as the probable full costs should be recognized at the outset when one is making decisions about building a house or a branch plant.

Another trouble with conventional government budgeting is the impact on lower-level incentives. Officials in the public as well as the private sectors maximize utility in view of whatever constraints they face. In a competitive industry lower-level officials and employers find it relatively rewarding to seek increased profits or reduced losses. In governmental units, officials often find it relatively rewarding to seek increased staffs and budgets, as suggested by Parkinson's law. To achieve these aims, they tend to use foot-in-the-door techniques—to get something started without calling attention to the full costs. Later, when part of the costs are sunk and the incremental costs are correspondingly lower, completion of the new venture may be economical from almost anyone's standpoint. Such behavior may be made comparatively rewarding or inexpensive to officials under conventional budgeting, that is, with one year's outlays organized in terms of inputs.

In all these instances, the ill effects are presumably reduced or kept in check by the bargaining process. Flagrant neglect of future costs (either deliberate or inadvertent) or gross neglect of interdependencies would bring psychic costs, harsh criticism, and other penalties; and some effort is therefore devoted to mitigating these undesirable effects. But it would probably be worthwhile to modify budgeting arrangements to make alleviating these ill effects less costly and not alleviating them more costly to individual officials.

program budgeting[1]

For many years there have been discussions of, and experimentation with, budgets in terms of categories that are more nearly like outputs. This type of exhibit was originally called a "performance budget," but nowadays is more

---

[1] For discussions of various aspects of program budgeting, see David Novick (ed.), *Program Budgeting*, Harvard University Press, Cambridge, Mass., 1965; Charles J. Hitch, *Decision-making for Defense*, University of California Press, Berkeley, Calif., 1965; Stephen Enke (ed.), *Defense Management*, Prentice-Hall, Inc., Englewood Cliffs, N.J., 1967.

frequently called a "program budget." At first the possibilities were explored with reference to municipal activities, but in 1961 the Department of Defense introduced a new program-budgeting system that proved to be relatively successful, and in 1965 many Federal agencies were directed to introduce similar procedures.[2] There is also growing interest in possible innovations along these lines in other countries and in state governments, universities, and other organizations.

Program budgeting may mean different things to different persons, for the label is sometimes used to cover any of several packages of features. The hallmarks of the program budget, however, are (1) the restructuring of the budget in terms of intermediate outputs or missions, and (2) the presentation of proposed costs for several years ahead. The categories are inevitably intermediate rather than ultimate or even penultimate outputs. It is not helpful to think in terms of such final products as national security, or good health, or satisfaction; for such amorphous categories there are no units about which we can think. In the Department of Defense, for example, the programs are broad missions, such as "Strategic and Retaliatory Forces," and the program elements are component capabilities, such as the Minuteman, Fleet Ballistic Missile (Polaris), and B-58 bomber systems. These are not ultimate outputs like "national security"; yet accumulating cost estimates for these capabilities appears to be more useful than presenting the costs of personnel, travel, and fuel across the board within a branch of the military service.

In addition to these two major features, the use of cost-benefit or cost-effectiveness analysis is often regarded as an integral part of program budgeting. The reason is that while the revised budget format calls attention to important trade-offs, and may make possible better subjective judgments about the allocation of resources, it (1) provides only very limited assistance by itself and (2) fits naturally with the use of quantitative analysis to help allocate resources among programs and program elements. In the latter part of this chapter, I shall discuss cost-benefit analysis as another economic calculus to aid economic efficiency, and, in the next chapter, I shall discuss some possible disadvantages or costs of program budgeting as a control instrument. At this point let us examine program budgeting that does not employ cost-effectiveness analysis and that serves merely as an information system.

The information provided by the revised budget format and process would tend to alleviate the difficulties mentioned earlier. That is, the existence of this information would reduce the costs of taking interdependencies into account and of considering the future cost implications of alternative decisions. Moreover, the existence of this information might improve incentives at lower levels

---

[2] U.S. Bureau of the Budget Bulletin 66-3, Oct. 12, 1965.

—by calling attention to inappropriate behavior, such as the foot-in-the-door tactic, and making such behavior more expensive from the viewpoints of lower-level personnel. Against these good effects, of course, one should weigh whatever costs are entailed by constructing and using the program budget.

But, as noted above, the value of the information provided by a program budget per se is rather limited.

First, just how useful a particular set of programs and program elements will be is not obvious. If the military academies are put under an education program, they cannot simultaneously be put in the defense program. If subsidies to medical students are put in an education program, they cannot at the same time be part of a health program. If desalinization efforts are included in a research and development program, they cannot be included, at least in the same exhibit, in the natural-resources program. The point is that many or even most activities relate to more than one intermediate output, and the best way to classify them to aid decision makers is not easy to perceive. As you make one choice easier, you make another one more difficult; as you direct attention to one set of trade-offs, you fail to highlight another set of trade-offs. Some persons feel that the structure should be altered at intervals to avoid the bureaucratic blindness that can arise with *any* specific program-element structure. In any event, a program-budget format will *not* be a panacea.

Moreover, while interdependencies among programs and program elements will be fewer and less difficult to perceive than interdependencies among across-the-board inputs, there will still be plenty of complex interrelationships. What one does about highway transportation may affect the costs or benefits from urban-development program elements or from natural-resource program elements such as smog control. What one decides about social security may affect the costs and gains from alternative adult-education activities. What actions are taken regarding irrigation and flood control may affect the gains and costs of beaches and other recreational facilities. To repeat: The advantages of an improved format are at best limited, and groping for the most useful set of programs and program elements is bound to take considerable time.

Second, the cost estimates for program elements are less meaningful than many people imagine. Allocating "overhead" or "common" costs can yield only a crude approximation of a program element's total cost. The costs of administrative staffs that serve a whole agency, or repair shops and facilities that serve numerous program elements, are likely to be allocated on an almost arbitrary basis. Some inputs, like petroleum and lubricants, can be managed better on an aggregate basis with the allocation among program elements left flexible, and any specific allocation is likely to be off the mark. Moreover, personnel at lower levels will have to supply many of the estimates, yet they may have an imperfect understanding of proper cost estimates or little incentive to provide them.

To complicate matters further, different agencies face different cost problems and handle them with different degrees of competence, so that the significance of cost estimates will vary from agency to agency.

Third, even if the total cost of a program element or the average cost per unit (for example, the cost per thousand Job Corps trainees) were accurate, it would still be only a crude approximation of incremental cost—the cost of the particular increment or decrement under consideration; yet it is incremental cost that is relevant to specific choices. Incremental costs in government activities depend upon the particular circumstances: Do administrative or servicing facilities really have to be expanded proportionately? Is some other activity being phased out so that certain installations would be inherited? Is the incremental activity to be located in the arctic, the tropics, or downtown Chicago?

Fourth, the program budget as such provides no clues to the effectiveness or benefits from increments to alternative program elements. By posing the right questions it presumably facilitates making judgments, but it still gives little help in gauging anticipated benefits.

Thus, the exhibits in the program budget—for example, the Five-Year Force Structure and Financial Program, often called "The Blue Book," in the U.S. Defense Department—may help officials make broad allocative decisions, yet the assistance given is quite limited. And these exhibits help hardly at all in making detailed management decisions. Among other things, these limitations suggest that (1) additional information about the costs and gains implied by alternative program choices will often be valuable (which is why many persons regard cost-benefit analysis as an integral part of a program-budgeting system) and (2) the usefulness of program budgeting as an economic calculus will vary from one activity to the next. Thus, in the Defense Department, program budgeting has proved to be more valuable in shaping strategic retaliatory forces than in reaching decisions about general-purpose forces. In some parts of government it may give almost no assistance—for example, in foreign-aid programs, which yield numerous incommensurable outputs, or in transportation programs, where interdependencies with the rest of the economy tend to dominate the picture.

Another limitation of the program budget as an information system is its own cost. In the Federal government, Congress is almost certain to retain one-year budgeting in more or less the conventional categories. In other governmental units, also, this is likely to be true, especially since some inputs are managed more effectively on an aggregate basis than program element by program element. As a consequence, the program budget will often be superimposed on the older budgetary apparatus, as it was in the U.S. Defense Department. This creates not only a mountain of paper work, but also quite a bit of conflict between the producers and users of the two budgets. Sometimes, if the two budget cycles are not in harmony, decisions in terms of program elements will be inconsistent with almost simultaneous decisions in terms of certain input categories that cut across many program elements.

A final limitation on program budgeting purely as an information system deserves special emphasis: It may have little or no impact on decisions. For a number of years, the U.S. Budget Bureau had something like a program budget for the budgetary exhibit called "Civil Works Proposals." It was organized in meaningful functions or outputs, it crossed departmental lines, it showed costs for six years or so ahead—and it apparently had no effect on choices! Had the new Defense Department budget been merely an information system without increased centralization of authority, it might have had virtually no impact on defense choices. The individual military services would have found it only a little more costly than before to take parochial viewpoints. To have decisions made in the light of a program budget *and enforced* may in the end require a reshuffling of authority and a change in the bargaining mechanism (which may itself entail some costs that will be examined in the next chapter).

cost-benefit analysis[3]

"Cost-benefit analyses" are attempts to estimate certain costs and gains that would result from alternative courses of action. For different applications, other names are often used: "cost-effectiveness analysis" when courses of action in defense planning are compared; "systems analysis" when the alternatives are relatively complex collections of interrelated parts; "operations research" when the alternatives are modes of operation with more or less given equipment and resources; or "economic analysis" when the alternatives are rival price-support or other economic policies. The term "cost-benefit analysis" was originally associated with natural-resource projects but has gradually come to be used for numerous other applications. The basic idea is not new: individuals have presumably been weighing the pros and cons of alternative actions ever since man appeared on earth; and in the early part of the nineteenth century, Albert Gallatin and others put together remarkably sophisticated studies of proposed U.S. government canals and turnpikes. But techniques have improved, and interest has been growing. All these studies might well be called economic analyses. This does not mean that the economist's skills are the only ones needed in

---

[3] For more detail on many of these points, see Charles J. Hitch and Roland N. McKean, *The Economics of Defense in the Nuclear Age*, Harvard University Press, Cambridge, Mass., 1960.

making such analyses or, indeed, that economists are very good at making them. It merely means that this analytical tool is aimed at helping decision makers— consumers, businessmen, or government officials—economize.

In recent years, the Bureau of the Budget, the National Bureau of Standards, many other U.S. agencies, and governments and agencies in other nations have been exploring possible uses of cost-benefit analysis.[4] Sometimes the analyses are essentially simple arithmetic. Sometimes high-speed computers are used—as they were, for instance, in the search by a Harvard group for the best way to use water in the Indus River basin in Pakistan. One of the major applications of cost-benefit analysis will continue to be the comparison of alternative natural-resources policies—proposals to reduce air and water pollution, to divert water from the Yukon to regions further south, to do something about the rapidly declining water level in the Great Lakes, and so on. But other applications are appearing with growing frequency—comparisons of such things as alternative health measures, personnel policies,[5] airport facilities, education practices, transportation systems, choices about the management of governmental properties, and antipoverty proposals.

All such analyses involve working with certain common elements: (1) objectives, or the beneficial things to be achieved; (2) alternatives, or the possible systems or arrangements for achieving the objectives; (3) costs, or the benefits that have to be foregone if one of the alternatives is adopted; (4) models, or the sets of relationships that help one trace out the impacts of each alternative on achievements (in other words, on benefits) and costs; and (5) a criterion, involving both costs and benefits, to identify the preferred alternative. In connection with each of these elements there are major difficulties. Consider a personal problem of choice that an individual might try to analyze—selecting the best arrangements for his family's transportation. Spelling out the relevant objectives, that is, the kind of achievements that would yield significant benefits, is no simple task. The objectives may include commuting to work, getting the children to school, travel in connection with shopping, cross-country trips, and so on. Part of this travel may be across deserts, along mountain roads, in rainy or icy or foggy conditions. The family may attach a high value to the prestige of traveling in style (or of being austere, or of simply being different from most other people). Another objective that is neglected all too often is a

---

[4] For pertinent references, see Alan R. Prest and Ralph Turvey, "Cost-Benefit Analysis: A Survey," *Economic Journal*, December, 1965, pp. 683–735. See also Robert Dorfman (ed.), *Measuring Benefits of Government Investments*, The Brookings Institution, Washington, D.C., 1965.

[5] Joseph A. Kershaw and Roland N. McKean, *Teacher Shortages and Salary Schedules*, McGraw-Hill Book Company, New York, 1962.

hard-to-specify degree of flexibility to deal with uncertainties. Adaptability and flexibility are particularly important objectives if one is examining alternative educational programs, exploratory research projects, or R&D policies. Overlooking any of the relevant objectives could lead to poor choices.

The second element, the alternative ways of achieving the benefits, also deserves careful thought, for selecting the best of an unnecessarily bad lot is a poor procedure. In choosing a family's transportation system, the alternatives might include various combinations of a compact automobile, a luxury automobile, a pickup truck, a jeep, a motor scooter, an airplane, a bicycle, the use of a bus system, and the use of taxicabs.

In many problems of choice, the alternatives are called "systems," and the analyses are called "systems analyses." This terminology is quite appropriate, because the word "system" means a set of interrelated parts, and the alternative ways of achieving objectives usually are sets of interrelated parts. At the same time, the word "system" is so general that this usage is often confusing. In defense planning, for example, the term "system" can be used to refer to such sets of interrelated parts as the following:

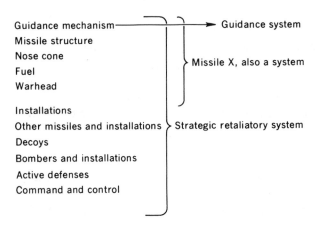

All three of these systems are collections of interrelated parts. How large should systems be for their comparison to be called a "systems analysis" or for their comparison to be a useful aid? There are no correct answers; one must exercise judgment in deciding how large the systems should be to provide worthwhile assistance in tracing out the costs and benefits. (In effect, one must weigh the costs against the benefits of preparing alternative cost-benefit analyses.) Where interrelationships are relatively important, one is usually driven to consider large systems. Thus to choose between two engines for a supersonic airliner, one can hardly compare thrusts alone and make an intelligent selection, for weight, reliability, cost, noise, etc., may have diverse effects on overall desirability. The power plants must be fitted (at least on paper) into rival aircraft designs, and thence into airline and airport systems to see their net impact on the real objectives and the full costs. Moreover, other components of the projected systems may have to be modified so as not to use either engine stupidly. Suppose one engine would make possible the use of relatively short runways. To use an aircraft with this power plant in an intelligent way, one might have to modify many parts of the proposed airports, traffic patterns, ground installations for instrument-landing systems, and even proposed airline schedules. Hence one would end up comparing rather broad systems having many common components but also having several components that differed.

So much for the alternative systems to be compared. The third element of cost-benefit analysis, cost, is crucial because it really reflects the alternative benefits that one might obtain from the resources. It is just as foolish to measure costs incorrectly or to neglect part of them as it is to measure benefits incorrectly or neglect part of them. If selecting a luxury car entails building a new garage or paying higher insurance premiums, these are part of the costs of choosing that alternative. If one already has an adequate garage, the value foregone by using it (but *not* the cost of building a garage) is the relevant cost.

"Models," the fourth element of cost-benefit analysis, are simply crude representations of reality that enable one to estimate costs and benefits. If a person figures, "With the bus I could average 10 miles per hour, traverse the 5 miles to work in one-half hour, spend five hours per week commuting to work, and would stand up 50 percent of the distance on 50 percent of the trips," he is using a model. If he says, "With Automobile X, I would get a motor tune-up every 5,000 miles and would therefore spend $50 per year on that item," he visualizes these events and uses a set of relationships, that is, a model, to estimate this cost. When one tries to perceive how something would work, it has become convenient and fashionable to say, "Let's build a model," though one could simply say, "Let's devise a way to predict what would happen (or a way to estimate costs and benefits)."

The fifth element of cost-benefit analysis is the criterion or test of preferredness by means of which one points to the best choice. People tend to make a variety of criterion errors.[6] One error, the use of the ratio of benefits to costs, is such a perennial favorite that it merits a brief discussion. Suppose at first that both benefits and costs can be measured *fully and correctly* in monetary terms

---

[6] Hitch and McKean, *op. cit.*, chap. 9.

and that one must choose among the following three discrete (and not mutually exclusive) alternatives:

	A	B	C
Cost	$100	$100	$200
Benefit one year later	$150	$105	$220
Ratio of benefits to costs	1.5	1.05	1.10

Suppose further that the constraint is that funds can be borrowed at 6 percent. Which projects should be undertaken, and what is the criterion? A and C, both of which yield more than 6 percent, should be undertaken, and the proper criterion is to maximize the present value of net worth or, its surrogate, to undertake projects wherever the marginal benefit exceeds the marginal cost. Note that the criterion is *not* to maximize the ratio of benefits to costs, which would restrict one to Project A. If the constraint is a fixed budget of $200, Projects A and B should be selected. Again, maximizing the ratio of benefits to costs would limit one to Project A.

Or consider two discrete and mutually exclusive alternatives (for example, two sizes of a dam):

	A	B
Cost	$100	$200
Benefit one year later	$150	$260
Ratio of benefits to costs	1.50	1.30

If funds can be borrowed at 6 percent, Project B should be undertaken. One should not choose A simply because the benefit-cost ratio is larger. Ratios are not irrelevant—every marginal productivity is a ratio—for one often seeks to *equalize* certain ratios as a condition for achieving a desired maximum. But the ratio itself is not the thing to be maximized.

The issue takes on a good deal of importance when the benefits can only be suggested by physical products or capabilities. In these circumstances, presumably in desperation, people frequently adopt as a criterion the maximization of some such ratio as satellite payload per dollar, hours of student instruction per dollar, or target-destruction capability per dollar. But the benefit-cost ratios of rival proposals simply cover up the relevant information. Take another example from the choices that confront the individual. If one is selecting a hose with which to sprinkle his lawn, one may have the following options:

	⅝-IN. DIAMETER	1-IN. DIAMETER
Cost	$3	$5
Benefit (water put on lawn per hour)	108 gallons	150 gallons
Ratio of benefits to costs	36/1	30/1

The ratios are irrelevant. The pertinent question is whether or not the extra capability is worth the extra $2. Less misleading than showing the ratio would be showing the physical capabilities and the costs à la consumers' research. Or, where it makes sense to do so, one can adjust the scale of the alternatives so that each costs the same or achieves the same objectives. Then one can see which system achieves a specified objective at minimum cost, or achieves the greatest benefit for a specified budget. This is not a perfect criterion, for someone has to decide if the specified budget (or objective) is appropriate. But at least this sort of test is less misleading than a benefit-cost ratio.

With regard to this fifth element of cost-benefit analysis, discussing the correct way to design criteria may seem like discussing the correct way to find the Holy Grail. In a world of uncertainty and individual utility functions, judgments must help shape choices, and no operational test of preferredness can be above suspicion. Moreover, analyses vary in their quality, which is hard to appraise, and in their applicability to different decisions. For these reasons, responsible decision makers must treat cost-benefit analyses as "consumers' research" and introduce heroic judgments in reaching final decisions. In a sense, then, it may be both presumptuous and erroneous to discuss having a test of preferredness in these quantitative analyses.

Criteria should be considered, nonetheless, in connection with such analysis. First, cost-benefit analysts do apply criteria, especially in designing and redesigning the alternatives to be compared. They delete features that appear to be inefficient, add features that appear to be improvements, and probe for alternative combinatio..s that are worth considering. This screening of possibilities and redesign of alternative systems entails the use of criteria, and these should be explicitly considered and exhibited. Second, whether or not they ought to, analysts often present the final comparisons in terms of a criterion. Thus while it may be wrong to talk as if a definitive criterion is an element of every analysis, these warnings about criterion selection should be emphasized.

Needless to say, in reaching decisions, one should attempt to take into account *all* gains and *all* costs. Some people feel that there are two types of gain or cost, economic and noneconomic, and that economic analysis has nothing to do with the latter. This distinction is neither very sound nor very useful. People pay for—that is, they value—music as well as food, beauty or quiet as well as aluminum pans, a lower probability of death as well as garbage disposal. The significant categories are not economic and noneconomic items but (1) gains and costs that can be measured in monetary units (for example, the use of items like typewriters that have market prices reflecting the marginal evaluations of all users); (2) other commensurable effects (impacts of higher teacher salaries, on the one hand, and of teaching machines, on the other hand, on students' test scores); (3) incommensurable effects that can be quantified but not in terms of a common denominator (capability of improving science test scores and capability of reducing the incidence of ulcers among students); and (4) nonquantifiable effects. Examples of the last category are impacts of alternative policies on the morale and happiness of students, on the probability of racial conflicts, and on the probability of protecting individual rights. In taking a position on an issue, each of us implicitly quantifies such considerations. But there is no way to make quantifications that would necessarily be valid for other persons. This sort of distinction between types of effects does serve a useful purpose, especially in warning us of the limitations of cost-benefit analysis.

One should recognize, too, that cost-benefit analysis necessarily involves groping and the making of subjective judgments, not just briskly proceeding with dispassionate scientific measurements. Consider the preparation of such analyses to aid educational choices. No one says, "This is the educational objective, and here are the three alternative systems to be compared. Now trace out the impacts of each on cost and on achievement of the objective, and indicate the preferred system." What happens is that those making the analysis spend much time groping for an *operational* statement of the objective, such as a designated improvement in specific test scores without an increase in the number of dropouts or nervous breakdowns. A first attempt is made at designing the alternative ways of realizing this objective. Preliminary costs are estimated. Members of the research team perceive that the systems have differential impacts on other objectives, such as flexibility, or student performance on tests two years later, or student interest in literature. Or the rival arrangements may elicit different reactions from teachers, parents, and school boards, affecting the achievement of other objectives. The analysts redesign the alternatives in the light of these impacts, perhaps so that each alternative performs at least "acceptably" with respect to each objective. Next it appears that certain additional features such as extra English-composition courses might add greatly to capability but not much to cost. Or the research team's cost group reports that certain facilities are extremely expensive and that eliminating them might reduce costs greatly with little impairment of effectiveness. In both cases the systems have to be modified again. This cut-and-try procedure is essential. Indeed, this process of redesigning the alternatives is probably a more important contribution than the final cost-effectiveness exhibits. In any event, the preparation of such an analysis is a process of probing—and not at all a methodical scientific comparison following prescribed procedures.

An appreciation of cost-benefit analysis also requires an awareness that incommensurables and uncertainties are pervasive. Consider the impacts of alternative educational policies that were mentioned above. These effects can perhaps be described, but not expressed in terms of a common denominator. Judgments about the extent of these effects and their worth have to be made. Some costs, such as the monetary measures of foregone benefits, perhaps additional sacrifices in terms of personality adjustment and ultimate effectiveness, or undesirable political repercussions that yield costs, cannot validly be put in terms of a common denominator. Furthermore, because of uncertainties, whatever estimates can be prepared should in principle be probability distributions rather than unique figures for costs and gains. The system that performs best in one contingency may perform worst in another contingency. Finally, costs and gains occur over a period of time, not at a single point in time, and there is no fully acceptable means of handling these streams of costs and gains in analyzing many options.[7]

These difficulties are present because life is complex, and there is no unique correct choice. The difficulties are not created by cost-benefit analysis. Moreover, they do not render quantitative economic analysis useless. They simply mean that one has to be discriminating about when and how to use various tools. In general, the broader choices made by higher-level officials pose relatively great difficulties regarding what value judgments to make and what the physical and social consequences of alternative actions would be. Consider, for example, the allocation of the U.S. budget among various departments or the allocation of funds among such functions as the improvement of health, education, or postal service. Cost-benefit analysis gives relatively little guidance in making these choices, for in the end the decision maker's task is dominated by difficult personal judgments. Cost-benefit analysis may help somewhat, for it is the appropriate framework in terms of which to *think* about these broad choices, and it can usually provide *some* improved information. When personal judgments must play such a huge role, however, the improved information may not be worth much.

Consider another example of such broad choices: the government's allocation of its R&D effort between basic research and applied development. To choose between these two alternatives, officials must rely heavily on personal

---

[7] For further discussion of the difficulties regarding incommensurables, uncertainties, and time streams, see Hitch and McKean, *op. cit.*, chaps. 10 and 11.

judgments about the consequences and judgments concerning the value of those consequences. Values cannot be taken as agreed upon, and physical-sociological effects cannot be predicted with confidence. Quantitative analysis can probably contribute only a little toward the sharpening of intuition here. Or consider the allocation of effort between improving medical care for the aged and improving it for the young. Suppose one could make extremely good predictions of the effects, which would of course aid decision makers. The final choice would be dominated in this instance by value judgments about the worth of prolonging the lives of elderly persons, the worth of lengthening the lives of persons in great pain, the worth of saving the lives of weakened or physically handicapped children, the relief of different kinds of distress, and so on.

Another broad or high-level choice that brings out these difficulties is the allocation of funds to, or for that matter within, the State Department. In the tasks of diplomacy it is hard to visualize taking a set of value tags as being clearly stated, let alone agreed upon. And disagreement is quite understandable in predicting the effects of alternative courses of action on the probabilities of stable alliances, provocations, little wars, nuclear wars, and so on. Positive science has provided few tested hypotheses about these relationships.

As one proceeds to narrower or lower-level problems of choice, these difficulties frequently, though not always, become less severe. (Actual decisions, of course, vary continuously in the extent to which they present these difficulties, but it is often economical to think in terms of such categories as broad and narrow or high-level and low-level choices). Within such tasks as education and health improvement, there are lower-level choices for which quantitative analysis may be very helpful, but there are also many middle-level choices that are fraught with difficulties. Should more effort be placed on the improvement of mental health even if it means less emphasis on the treatment of conventional ailments? Should effort be reallocated from higher education toward the improvement of elementary-school training, or vice versa? Or, as an alternative policy, should government leave such allocative decisions more than at present to the uninfluenced choices of individual families? Cost-benefit analysis cannot do much to resolve the uncertainties about the consequences of such decisions, about their relative worths to individual citizens, or about whose value judgments should be given what weights.

Within applied research and development, a choice between specific projects might appear to be a low-level choice that economic analysis could greatly assist. In such instances, it is true that values can sometimes be taken as agreed upon. In selecting research and development projects for new fuels, for instance, the values to be attached to various outcomes are not obvious, yet they are probably not major sources of divergent views. Perhaps the principal difficulty is the inability to predict the physical consequences, including "side effects," of alternative proposals. Here too, cost-benefit analysis may be destined to play a comparatively small role.

One can list many problems of choice that seem to fall somewhere in this middle ground—that is, where cost-benefit analysis can be helpful but not enormously so. It would appear, for instance, that the selection of antipoverty and welfare programs depends heavily on consequences that one cannot predict with confidence and on value judgments about which there is much disagreement. Similar statements apply also to the selection of foreign-aid programs, urban-development proposals, or law-enforcement programs—the comparison of different methods of curbing the use of narcotics, say, or of different penal institutions and procedures. In education, many decisions that may appear to be low-level or relatively simple—for example, the selection among alternative curricula or teaching methods or disciplinary rules—are inevitably dominated by judgments about the consequences of these policies and about the value tags to be attached to those consequences.

It is in connection with comparatively narrow problems of choice that cost-benefit analysis can sometimes play a more significant role. In these instances, as might be expected, the alternatives are usually rather close substitutes. Science can often predict the consequences of governmental natural-resource investments or choices affecting the utilization of water or land, and people can often agree on the values at stake—at least to a sufficient extent to render analyses highly useful. Competing irrigation plans, flood-control projects, swamp drainage and land reclamation ventures, and water-pollution control measures are examples of narrow problems of choice in which cost-benefit analysis can help.

Cost-benefit analysis also promises to be helpful in comparing certain transportation arrangements. The interdependencies of transportation networks with other aspects of life are formidable, yet with ingenuity extremely useful studies of some transportation alternatives can be produced.[8] Numerous transportation alternatives have been the subject of such studies: highways, urban systems, inland waterways, modified railway networks, the utilization of a given amount of sea transport, air transport fleets, and of couse many lower-level choices, such as alternative road materials, construction practices, airport facilities, and loading arrangements. In some instances, of course, the interdependencies may be too complex for analyses to be very valuable; transportation alternatives that

[8] See especially J. R. Meyer, J. F. Kain, and M. Wohl, *The Urban Transportation Problem*, Harvard University Press, Cambridge, Mass., 1965; and T. M. Coburn, M. E. Beesley, and D. J. Reynolds, *The London-Birmingham Motorway: Traffic and Economics*, Road Research Laboratory Technical Paper 46, D.S.I.R., H.M. Stationery Office, London, 1960.

affect a large region and its development yield chains of consequences that are extremely difficult to trace out.

At best, the difficulties of providing *valuable* information are awesome. As stressed in Chapter 3, there can always be legitimate disagreement about any of these policy decisions, and analyses must be regarded as inputs to decisions, not as oracular touchstones. Nonetheless, to think systematically about the costs and gains from alternative policies is surely more sensible than to rely on haphazard thought or intuition. Such analyses can bring out the areas of disagreement so that people can see where their differences lie. Even with considerable divergence in judgments, they can screen out the absurdly inferior alternatives, focusing the debate on subsets of relatively good alternatives. For some choices, cost-benefit analysis provides information that can help officials agree upon a course of action that is preferred or accepted by most citizens. And for all choices, it is the right framework to use in organizing the evidence and one's thoughts and intuitions regarding alternatives. Even in deciding which research project to undertake, or how much time to spend on it, a researcher consults rough cost-benefit T-accounts. In deciding anything, a person should weigh costs and gains. Preliminary weighing may suggest that the use of a tentative rule of thumb or "requirement" is preferable to further or repeated analyses, but he should not initially pull some mythical requirement out of the air.

nine

Chapter 8 considered the possible contribution of improved economic calculations to efficiency in government—efficiency in terms of one's preferences or in terms of whatever actions would be sanctioned by the decision-making rules he accepts. As noted in Chapter 2, however, even a relevant calculus is impotent if the unseen hand permits or even compels decision makers to ignore such calculations. To get more from given resources (of whatever is wanted from government), it is important to consider the use of *both* better information *and* improved institutional arrangements. In Chapter 9, therefore, let us turn to the consideration of some modifications of the institutional framework and their possible impacts.

As indicated in the earlier discussions, it is assumed that individuals are utility maximizers. If something becomes more rewarding, they will demand more of that and less of other things. If something becomes more costly, they will trade some of that item for other things. (Both rewards and costs include all kinds of pecuniary and nonpecuniary considerations.) In government as in the private sector, one would like to encourage actions that one regards as desirable and discourage those one deems to be undesirable. One would therefore like an institutional framework that penalized decision makers for taking the undesirable actions and rewarded them for taking the desirable steps. Economics has had much more to say about the institutional framework than about cost-gain calculations in the private sector, partly because with the proper framework only those firms that made certain kinds of calculations and decisions would survive. Economics should give a good deal of attention to the institutional framework in the public sector also.[1]

As noted in Chapter 7, my application of demand theory to behavior in the public sector is speculative because I may not perceive what really happens to the costs to individuals of the indicated forms of behavior. As more centralization occurs, for example, other things may not remain constant. One force may make certain types of behavior relatively expensive, but other forces that I fail to perceive may work in the opposite direction. Nonetheless, while most of the conclusions are speculative, I do feel some confidence that this way of thinking about alternative institutional arrangements will prove to be useful.

the gains and costs of increased centralization[2]

One feature of government decision making that inevitably impresses people is its fragmented nature and the pervasiveness of interdependencies. Different persons use different terminology to refer to this difficulty: for example, they speak of the existence of externalities or spillovers, the ill effects of suboptimization or parochial viewpoints, or perhaps just the lack of coordination. Regardless of terminology, though, it is natural—when one realizes how many Federal and other agencies engage in activities affecting health or natural resources or education—to conclude that someone with an overall viewpoint should make the interrelated decisions. A recognition of the disadvantages or costs of decentralization is one of several forces propelling us toward a greater degree of centralization.

The trouble is that centralization also entails costs, and these costs often take forms that are harder to recognize than the costs of fragmented decision making. The neglect of these costs can cause us to err in the direction of excessive centralization and to believe that ever-greater centralization is appropriate. Actually, as in applying other tools or inputs, applying centralization up to a point brings greater gains than costs but beyond that point brings greater

[1] For a number of related arguments, see David Braybrooke and Charles E. Lindblom, *A Strategy of Decision*, The Free Press of Glencoe, New York, 1963.

[2] In the first two sections I am indebted to James R. Schlesinger of the RAND Corporation for numerous discussions of these topics when we were both studying the implications of program budgeting.

costs than gains. Moreover, how far to go no doubt varies according to the particular problem of choice and situation.

Before examining the sacrifices or costs entailed by increased centralization, perhaps we should try to clarify the meaning of this term, for it is an ambiguous one. If "more authority" is given to middle-level officials, leaving less authority in the hands of both lower-level and top-level officials, does it constitute a step toward centralization or toward decentralization? Furthermore, "degree of authority" is a slippery concept. If the responsibility for certain additional decisions is given to an official but at the same time the responsibility for other decisions is taken from him, what has happened to his authority? But let us here confine our attention to instances of "dominance"—undiluted upward shifts of decision-making power—which we could all agree were increases in centralization. What kind of sacrifices or costs are entailed?

As in the preceding chapter, some notion of "correct" choice is implied, since the subject is again costs, benefits, and improvements. The standard that lurks behind the scenes is the set of choices that would be correct from the standpoint of any individual, such as the reader, or the set that would be implied by an accepted decision-making rule. The concern here will be with the effects of undiluted centralization on costs and benefits in terms of such a standard.

If this were a world of costless information, that is, a world of certainty, the sacrifice entailed by centralization might be zero. Voters, congressmen, and other participants in the whole process could costlessly identify whatever decisions would be called for by the agreed-upon decision-making rule. Officials could be penalized for incorrect choices and rewarded for correct ones. "Right" would be done. A high degree of centralization would be appropriate. In our world of vast uncertainties, however, increased centralization will, beyond some point, bring increasing costs, especially in the long run.

First let us examine the forces at work (that is, the changes in cost-reward structures confronting officials) and then turn to the consequences. Suppose, to take an extreme example, that the Director of the Budget had almost complete control over resource-allocation decisions in the U.S. government. His word would be law; he would have to reckon with virtually no one, bargain with no one. Assume further that he would delegate many decisions to trusted confederates (though not to agency heads) but would himself have tremendous ability and vitality. In these extreme circumstances, choices would be tailored to essentially one view of the future and one utility function. If he had to bargain with other officials, he would find it costly, from his own standpoint, to ignore other views. Since he would not have to reckon with others, however, the costs he would feel from neglecting views and preferences other than his own would decline, and he would take more of this "item."

Another shift in the cost-reward structure facing our hypothetical Director of the Budget is that the costs of careful decision making would go up (or, alternatively, his rewards from simplifying choice-making procedures would increase) because of the tremendous burden of decisions placed upon him. In other words he would now find it advantageous—indeed, imperative—to screen alternatives rapidly, apply crude rules of thumb and quick judgments, and in general simplify his decision-making process, because he would have to make 1,000 instead of 100 decisions per day.

The costs and rewards facing personnel at lower levels, say in the individual departments, would shift also. They would now find it less rewarding than before to ponder alternative ways of performing tasks, since they would not make the choices anyway. They would probably find it less rewarding (or actually costly) to propose and fight for new ideas, because, in the new milieu and without bargaining power, they would not find their proposals accepted very often. For similar reasons they would find it relatively unrewarding (or positively costly) to criticize other agencies or to disagree with the Budget Bureau. In general they would now find it relatively advantageous to concentrate on implementing the Budget Bureau's decisions insofar as these were unambiguous and enforceable and on analyzing only those particular choices that were still open to them.

Now let us consider the probable consequences of these shifts in individual costs and rewards. One major consequence would be that the forces described above could cause fewer alternatives to be examined than before. The dominance of *one* view of the future and of *one* utility function, and the premium attached to simplified choice making, would cause many courses of action to be overlooked entirely, discarded immediately, or given only half-serious consideration. As for lower-level agencies, they would spend less effort "looking for business" if their efforts almost never yielded any business anyway. Generally speaking, rivalry among agencies—the threat of one agency's introducing an innovation that would encroach on another agency's activity—is more effective than good intentions in preventing promising alternatives from being overlooked. The Navy's Polaris probably played a larger role than good analysis and a broad viewpoint in arousing Air Force interest in reducing the vulnerability of Minuteman. Rivalry among such agencies as the Department of the Interior, the Department of Agriculture, and the Corps of Engineers has helped direct at least a little attention to unconventional sources of water, such as the reclaiming of sewage and the reduction of evapotranspiration from reservoirs and canals.

Consider another activity that may gradually become more highly centralized —the provision of higher education. The major forces pushing toward centralization here are probably (1) the wish to provide low-tuition education, which brings tremendous expansion of state college-university systems and reduces the role of private universities, and (2) the reluctance of state legislatures or other governmental authorities to deal with numerous chancellors or university managements. (Above enrollments of 10,000 or so, the saving of legislators' time and effort may be one of the few economies of scale.) Because of centralization, students and faculty have fewer options in their region, and "voting with their feet" for the type of university they prefer becomes more expensive. The fact that "voting with their feet" becomes more expensive may not only reduce the range of alternatives available (in comparison with having independent rival universities) but also aggravate conflict. Each faction may begin to fight for the right to use university assets as it wishes. It is as though those customers and employees who disliked the policies of General Motors registered their disapproval by trying to run the business instead of by shifting to other firms.

Out of such situations, it might be noted, peculiar hybrid organizations often emerge. In state education systems there has on occasion developed what might be called "strangulated centralization." There is centralization in the sense of monopoly (a reduction in the role played by independent rivals) yet dispersal of power among faculty committees or even student groups. This is a very different dispersal of power from the sort that would exist with smaller autonomous competing universities or school systems. Again it is somewhat as though General Motors were the sole automobile manufacturer—paid by the state and with little reason to cater to consumers' or workers' demands—and operated by a ceaselessly shifting coalition of administrators, employee committees, and consumer committees.

To return to the main point, though, catering to a majority by means of a single university system or government agency would lead to less diversity (that is, the consideration of fewer alternatives) than having several rival units catering to the majorities in various smaller groups. The basic reason is that the unseen hand, the cost-reward structures confronting busy legislators and other central authorities, pulls officials in that direction.

A closely related consequence of increased centralization is the possible loss of flexibility and adaptability. Essentially, this loss takes the form of slowness in giving serious consideration to alternatives and is therefore closely related to, or is a special case of, the matter just discussed. When authority is highly centralized, there are numerous layers of officials. Given this form of organization, carefully prescribed procedures become economical. Exceptions to rules must themselves be spelled out as rules, for capricious exceptions would leave top administrators with little information about what was happening. Even routine decisions take a surprising amount of time, because personnel usually find that being wrong or failing to consult coadministrators is more costly to them than being slow. For nonroutine decisions it is doubly difficult and time-consuming to get approval or indeed to get any decision at all. With highly centralized authority, lower levels find it costly "to stick their necks out"; they are reluctant to give any guidance in advance of a formal written proposal, may find things wrong with the formal proposal one item at a time and return it for emendation, and refer most choices to higher authority. With enough effort, wooing, or screaming, favorable decisions can often be obtained without great delay, the cost in such instances taking the form of effort devoted to aggressive action rather than of delay or unfavorable decisions. In any event, flexibility and adaptability are made more costly to utility-maximizing officials, a sacrifice to be weighed against the gains from centralization.

Another cost of increased centralization is the neglect of relevant effects of the alternatives that are considered. The forces mentioned earlier—the dominance of one or a few views of the future, the dominance of one or a few utility functions, the value to the central authority of simplified procedures for choosing, the increased passivity of lower-level personnel—lead to the neglect of costs or gains felt by persons other than the central decision makers. The convenience of unified salary schedules, of rules against promoting persons without Ph.D.'s, of rules against hiring anyone working for his doctorate as a consultant, of agreements not to compete[3]—such impacts on convenience or administrative burdens are felt; but losses in the quality of teaching and research may not be felt by the central authority, unless they become sufficiently marked for someone with bargaining power to fight. The main point is that with increased centralization, decision makers are exposed to less dissent and criticism and fewer bargaining pressures. (With "strangulated centralization" they are exposed to special types of dissent and bargaining pressures.) Unless decision makers are super-beings, fewer of the relevant considerations will be aired than would be with a larger set of competing decentralized decision makers. Genuine gains and sacrifices entailed by alternative courses of action can more easily be neglected.

One consideration especially may be neglected, namely, the inherent uncertainties about the outcomes from alternative courses of action. If choices are shaped by one view of the future, if the simplification of procedures for choosing becomes relatively valuable to the chooser, if lower-level officials find it unrewarding to point out uncertainties, the central administrator finds fewer penalties and larger rewards attached to overlooking doubts. Criticism and dissent often bring to light the chances of alternative outcomes. The rivalry between the Department of Agriculture and the Corps of Engineers helped reveal the uncertainties about the effectiveness and costs of big dams versus numerous little dams for flood prevention. With respect to educational policies, proponents of any one view are often very dogmatic. The clash of diverse views

---

[3] J. F. Barron, "Restrictive Hiring Practices in Institutions of Higher Learning in California," *Journal of Law and Economics*, October, 1961, pp. 186–193.

reveals the extent of the uncertainties. If the proponents of any one view were solely responsible for policies, these uncertainties would tend to be neglected.

There is another way in which lower-level personnel may be induced to neglect uncertainties. Not only will they find it less rewarding (with a higher degree of centralization) to call attention to uncertainties about rival or official policies. In addition, they are likely to find it more rewarding to adopt a conservative bias, insofar as they continue to make proposals, than would otherwise be the case. With a relatively high degree of centralization, agencies probably face fewer threats of innovations by rival groups and greater reprimands for making mistakes. Hence they find it relatively advantageous to confine themselves to "safe" proposals and to neglect courses of action whose outcomes are highly uncertain even when those courses of action promise great rewards if they are successful.

Perhaps I should reemphasize that these remarks merely point to some costs of increased centralization. They do not indicate how much centralization would be appropriate in various circumstances any more than pointing to the cost of books indicates how many books one should buy in various circumstances. If one overlooks or underestimates these costs, however, he will buy too many books or too much centralization. It might be noted that complete centralization is prohibitively expensive; indeed the cost is infinite, because it is simply impossible for all authority to be in one person's hands. (Everyone recognizes these costs when he considers such hypothetical extremes.) For this reason, what appears on paper to be extreme centralization may turn out to contain dimly understood elements of decentralization—that is, to involve delegation of authority to new and dimly perceived groups.[4]

These costs of centralization vary with the type of decision. Where there is particularly great uncertainty—for example, in choosing among research and development projects or educational policies—it is especially costly to society to neglect alternatives, to reduce adaptability, or to blind oneself to uncertainty. Increased centralization in the planning of these activities brings particularly high total costs. Where there are fewer uncertainties or more crucial interdependencies, as in the actual conduct of military or postal operations with a given technology, a high degree of centralization may bring fewer costs and more gains.

This discussion has not pointed to a blueprint for desirable institutional arrangements. But it has tried to focus attention on some relevant and perhaps neglected considerations. When pondering alternative organizational schemes, one should try to perceive the often subtle ways in which organization affects the costs and rewards confronting officials and other personnel. One should

---

[4] See John C. Ries, *The Management of Defense*, The Johns Hopkins Press, Baltimore, 1964.

remember that competition within the public sector can be a powerful force pushing personnel in certain directions, and centralization can produce forces leading in other directions.

program budgeting as an instrument of control

In the preceding chapter, program budgeting was discussed purely as a device for producing information and aiding an official in making his economic calculus pertaining to alternative courses of action. But it was mentioned that better calculations from some overall standpoint may have little impact on actual decisions. It is often suggested therefore that program budgeting can accomplish something only when combined with increased centralization and that program budgeting must perforce lead to or facilitate centralization. If it does lead to centralization, the long-run costs or disadvantages of such centralization should be kept in mind in choosing the design and scope of the program-budgeting system.

It is by no means clear that such a budgeting system would itself be responsible for any centralization. It might have little effect on decisions, and perhaps wither away, in the absence of increased central authority. By the same token, however, the existence of the information contained in such a budget would probably have little impact on the decisions about centralization. The latter are largely separate decisions, prompted by costs and rewards as felt by the decision makers. Greater central authority would be decided upon, and could be introduced, with or without program budgeting. Other devices could be used to facilitate central decision making and to ensure compliance by lower levels.

Nonetheless, program budgeting may make it less costly to officials to centralize authority, and in any event entails some costs if it is effective. For example, to curb lower-level officials' use of the foot-in-the-door tactic, they may be held to the five-year cost estimates recorded in the program budget and forced to cut a program (or some other activity) if their original cost estimates prove to be too low. This appears to be a good thing, yet it may also bring a cost to society—the sacrifice, to some extent, of flexibility. That is, curbing the use of the foot-in-the-door technique almost necessarily makes it a little more difficult (costly from individual officials' standpoints) to effect changes in programs, and this reduction in adaptability is a cost from the standpoint of persons other than the officials.

Another force in operation when a five-year program is used as an instrument of control is the overt commitment of top officials to the choices recorded for the five-year period. Changes become more costly from a psychological as well as an administrative standpoint once these views of higher-level officials and promises to lower-level officials are on record. The taking of positions and the creation of vested interests five years ahead instead of for a shorter period is thus another factor reducing adaptability. Or, as some have suggested, there is a sort of Gresham's law of programming: whatever is recorded in the program tends to drive out the other options, and the longer the period covered, the greater the extent to which decisions based on little information drive out decisions based on more information.

Throughout this chapter, it might be reemphasized, I am merely indicating some costs that should be weighed against the gains of expanding our use of certain institutional arrangements. I am not condemning these devices, and I cannot indicate the extent to which they should be employed. All I can say is that in deciding how to design and how far to apply such organizational "inputs," these costs should not be neglected. Similarly, one might remind a firm (if it needed reminding) that garage facilities for trucks cost something and that, in deciding what kind of trucks and how many to employ, these components of total costs should be considered.

charging prices for governmental outputs

In the use of resources by government, one major difficulty arises from the fact that many goods and services dispensed by governmental agencies are provided free of charge—to individual consumers, to communities, or to other agencies in government. As might be expected, the users demand the service as long as the utility of another unit exceeds the cost *to them*. If the price is zero, they demand the item as long as another unit is worth more than zero, which means that people consume many units whose worth is less than the actual cost. That is, they consume units that they value less than they would value other things that could have been produced with those resources. If the items are rationed by lot, queues, arbitrary judgments, the difficulty of filling out applications, or any device other than price, consumption will not be pushed until the marginal worth is zero, but special costs are generated, and the goods will be awarded to some persons who don't consider them very important and denied to others who attach relatively high values to the items.

For example, if water is provided free of charge, it will be used carelessly; if there are free telephone lines between UCLA and Berkeley, they will be used as long as the utility of phone calls exceeds the congestion costs; if flood-control projects or inland waterways are provided to communities virtually free of charge, communities will be scrambling to have the Corps of Engineers build them; if army uniforms or typewriters or tape recorders are available upon requisition, they will be used liberally and cared for poorly. To reduce the waste or inefficient allocation of resources, special constraints (for example, only ten typewriters per department; only persons above a certain rank and with the approval of designated officials can obtain tape recorders) and also exhortation are often employed. But exhortation is rarely effective—why should I take good care of my equipment or use stationery sparingly when nobody else does?—and special constraints bring their own inefficiences and problems. So the possibilities of charging appropriate prices for many governmental services should be considered.

For many items dispensed to individuals, such as government publications, government-owned timber, and government-produced electric power, there have been user charges for a long time (though often below cost). Serious consideration is sometimes given to the adoption of user charges for more of our recreation services; rights to inject pollutants into streams; prospecting permits; oil, gas, mineral, and mining claims; and even inland waterways and radio frequencies. For services now provided at a price—such as grazing privileges, some of our recreational facilities, and water for irrigation—there is talk of making those prices more nearly a function of the amount consumed and more nearly equal to cost. For goods and services that have been provided to *regions* or *communities* below cost or free of charge, such as flood-control measures or recreational features of multipurpose projects, there is serious debate about charging higher fees *to these groups*—that is, of sharing project costs with them —as a condition for building such facilities. Each group would then have to worry about ways to tax or charge individuals; in the case of regional public goods such as flood control, it would often be prohibitively expensive to exclude individuals and charge them according to the amount of flood control they used, so the group would have to resort to assessments.

In addition, there is increased discussion of, and experimentation with, the charging of prices to other governmental units who use one agency's output. This has been done quite a bit in the Defense Department through the use of "stock and industrial funds," which set up certain supply operations (such as the provision of medical supplies, petroleum products, and indeed all the items handled by the Defense Supply Agency) and certain "manufacturing" or service operations (such as the provision of printing services, dry cleaning, and even sea and air transport services) as though they were business firms. They charge prices to their customers, so that governmental units desiring these supplies or services must buy them instead of merely requisitioning them. *If they could put the funds to some other use*, the users would feel a sacrifice or cost when buying these items and would be motivated to use them economically. There are, of course, limitations to and costs of using stock and industrial funds[5]—chiefly the difficulty of making these prices behave flexibly and appropriately. For example, it is hard to rig these prices to reflect benefits or costs to government units other than the users of the fund's output; and such externalities are pervasive within certain sectors of government.

While there is much interest in the use of these various devices, there is hardly a clear-cut trend toward charging prices for governmental outputs. For at the same time there is a growing tendency to provide certain goods and services—medical care and higher education are examples—below cost or free of charge. Moreover, it is not obvious that these particular arrangements for marketing public outputs should be adopted on a large scale. There are costs associated with the collection of user charges or with setting up any market devices. As usual, the burden of the argument here is simply that there is rarely such a thing as free lunch: a person should not ignore the sacrifices entailed by *any* of the alternative arrangements. In deciding upon his position, he should weigh the costs and advantages of stock funds, industrial funds, user charges, and cost sharing with local governments against the costs and advantages of providing various government outputs free of charge.

other institutional modifications

Dissatisfaction with public spending decisions has led to discussion, and use, of many other variations in the institutional framework. Every new bureau, every minor reorganization, every change in the system of checks and balances, every new directive or constraint—all these affect the bargaining mechanism, the cost-reward structures confronting various officials, and decisions about governmental use of resources. Let us examine two phenomena, "value engineering" and "incentive contracts," that seem to merit special attention.

Value engineering. Value engineering, sometimes called "de-goldplating," refers to systematic efforts to substitute less expensive components for more expensive ones, wherever they will enable equipment to perform just as well (or almost as well) as before.[6] Thus value engineering simply means a special set of attempts to economize—to find ways of reducing the costs of carrying out specified functions. It could be regarded as a special case of applying cost-effective-

---

[5] For further discussion of this topic, and of other points pertaining to institutional arrangements, see Charles J. Hitch and Roland N. McKean, *The Economics of Defense in the Nuclear Age*, Harvard University Press, Cambridge, Mass., 1960, and Atheneum Press, 1965, chap. 12.

[6] There is an extensive literature on value engineering, but I am especially indebted to an unpublished study by Dr. Allen C. Kelley of the University of Wisconsin.

ness or cost-benefit analysis. In a number of instances, fairly large savings have been made by discovering that cheaper components could serve fully as well as expensive ("gold-plated") ones. For example, using hydraulic jacks instead of a mechanism called a "mule" for opening and closing Minuteman silos is said to have saved over a million dollars. The substitution of plastic caps for metal ones on certain containers is supposed to have effected huge savings without impairing effectiveness.

To encourage the search for such economies, the U.S. government, chiefly the Defense Department, has set up in-house value-engineering groups, and the government sometimes agrees to share with contractors any eligible savings discovered by the latter. Moreover, the government often awards contracts on condition that the contractors set up value-engineering departments or spend specified amounts, or percentages of contracts, on value engineering. The Federal government has done this not only in contracts for the production of known items but also in many contracts for research and development. Enthusiastic advocates have hailed value engineering as an enormously important innovation and have claimed that it can save the United States billions of dollars.

Needless to say there is a good deal of waste in purchasing "gold-plated" items, and some degree of effort to cut costs in this way is no doubt economical. Here too, however, it should be recognized that this remedy itself entails significant costs that should be weighed against the prospective gains. First, it uses resources, mainly engineers, in large quantities. Second, value-engineering departments and value-engineering contracts may not really do much to counteract the other forces at work. Such departments may have little impact if neither government agencies nor contractors reap any take-home rewards from de-goldplating. Even if they reap such rewards, as contractors do under share-the-savings contracts, this may have only a slight influence on the overall incentive structure that is shaped by the competition among contractors. After all, agency personnel seek to maximize utility in total, not just efficiency in the design of products; and contractors are interested in present worth in total, not just the profits on particular contracts. Third, to the extent that value-engineering contracts do affect decisions, they tend to reduce flexibility, because in order to separate eligible savings from changes in costs caused by other factors, there must be careful bookkeeping on all changes in the product. Engineering change proposals must be submitted to government authorities for approval, and adaptability is made more costly to decision makers. In particular, trade-offs between cost and performance—substitutions that increase (or decrease) *both* cost and performance—may be neglected. Especially in the case of R&D contracts, this loss of flexibility may be manifested in longer production time and delayed delivery dates. Fourth, the sharing of value-engineering savings is sometimes written into *incentive* contracts, and these contractual provisions partially offset each other. (Part of the bonuses from de-goldplating would have been reaped from cost reduction relative to target costs anyway.) Fifth, contractors and in-house producers are given an incentive to gold-plate proposed products, or at least to neglect good design, initially in order to de-goldplate the products later on. Sixth, when an item costing $1 is substituted for another item costing $5, the net saving is not necessarily $4, because the change may entail other costs, such as new inventories, catalogs, training manuals, and maintenance manuals.

Thus there are a number of costs associated with value engineering that are all too easily neglected. In deciding where and how to use this technique, and how far to press its use, one should struggle to weigh the true costs against the true gains. Some of the enthusiasm for value engineering smacks once more of trying to increase efficiency regardless of cost!

Incentive contracts. Another part of the institutional framework that deserves special attention comprises the various kinds of incentive contracts. Experimentation with these devices, too, has been mainly in the Defense Department, but the possible use of incentive contracts will be a matter of increasing concern in various governmental units. The disadvantages of cost-plus-fixed-fee contracts are well known; so, even for research and development, governments have tried out new arrangements. Two types are especially worth noting: incentive-fee contracts and multidimensional incentive contracts.

In general terms, the former arrangement makes the fee smaller if an agreed-upon target cost is exceeded and larger if the cost is less than the target. It may seem that such contracts would unquestionably increase overall efficiency, and yet here too whatever gains are achieved do not come free of charge. In pondering the effects of such contracts, the principles to remember are: (1) Contractors and government officials, like the rest of us, expand activities that yield relatively high rewards and neglect actions that yield relatively small rewards; and (2) contractors try to maximize the present worth of their utility streams in total, not profits on particular contracts or the worth of particular utility streams. With an incentive-fee contract, what turns out to be relatively rewarding? As far as the contract itself is concerned, resources devoted to bargaining for a high target, to reducing costs, and to producing whatever *is* specified about the product are relatively rewarding. Care in getting approval of whatever changes *are* proposed is rewarding, but considering very many changes—adaptability in general—is relatively unrewarding. Attention to aspects of quality that are not spelled out in the contract is relatively unrewarding as far as the specific contract is concerned, but it may still be quite important from the contractor's standpoint. Why? Because the competition for *subsequent* profitable contracts, at least in the existing milieu, makes attention to quality and timeliness pay off despite the specific contractual provisions.[7] (In centrally planned countries, the counterpart of incentive contracts is often present; but there is not as much competition for future contracts, and aspects of quality or features of the product that do not yield premiums are more often neglected.)

Thus the incentive-fee contract brings some costs—the diversion of resources to bargaining about the target, reductions in adaptability, possibly the sacrifice of some aspects of quality—but competition, even if it appears to be far from vigorous in some respects, prevents the more absurd exchanges of unspecified performance for specified target hitting. With at least moderate competition, incentive-fee contracts may well yield a somewhat improved set of incentives or cost-reward structures.

The multidimensional incentive contract attempts to reward achievements along several dimensions, providing bonuses not only for cutting costs but also for accelerating delivery dates and for improving quality or performance (relative to agreed-upon targets in each instance). Sometimes the targets are tied to the *i*th output in a series of outputs, such as the tenth missile or the third atomic reactor bearing serial number so-and-so. Sometimes the targets are tied to components of the equipment being developed or produced. Again the effect of these bonuses, like the effect of value-engineering contracts, is tempered by the effect of the competition for future profitable contracts. To the extent that these multidimensional contracts influence decisions, however, they are likely to produce several ill effects or costs, especially when they apply to the development of new systems. The principal reason is that they will draw effort to those achievements that turn out to be relatively rewarding and away from important aspects of quality that do not yield bonuses. If the trade-offs could be specified in advance completely and correctly (e.g., desired and also feasible trade-offs between increases in the speed, reliability, and ease of maintenance of a new piece of equipment), the contract would not have ill effects. But they cannot be so specified. For one thing, these trade-offs are not linear, and they are not constant. For another thing, one cannot know in advance, at least in R&D, what trade-offs one would be willing to make or what trade-offs are technologically possible. With the contract drawn up, the contractor shifts his effort as he learns which achievements are easier, but the government adheres to the trade-offs implied in the contract. The contractor may be induced to concentrate his effort on bargaining for targets, on a particular serial number, on a particular component, or on particular aspects of performance. He may be induced to "storm" (as it is called in the U.S.S.R.) to deliver a quota on a par-

---

[7] For a thorough treatment of this and related subjects, see Frederic M. Scherer, *The Weapons Acquisition Process: Economic Incentives*, Harvard Graduate School of Business Administration, Boston, 1964.

ticular date, with too little regard for the impact on storage costs, future output, or quality. He may be led to sacrifice desirable changes and flexibility because of the increased difficulties of getting engineering-change proposals approved.

In conclusion, I stress the same old point. In most circumstances, the more extensively this technique or any other "input" is applied, the greater the incremental cost and the smaller the incremental gain. The institutional framework is extremely important, and in applying various modifications one should take a hard look at both the costs and the gains. The pasture on the other side of the fence often seems to be greener, but one should ceaselessly inquire: How much greener, and how much does it cost?

ten

MULTILEVEL GOVERNMENT AND
PUBLIC SPENDING

Public expenditures are made by numerous levels of
government—Federal, state, county, municipal, spe-
cial-district, and other public authorities. The allocation of powers and spending authority among
such governmental units is an extremely important
aspect of the institutional framework. Different arrangements lead to different outcomes, affecting not
merely material benefits but also other values resulting from the alternatives we choose—crucial
things like the degree of conflict in our society, the
manner in which conflicts are resolved, and the extent of individual freedom.

How should resources, or responsibilities, be allocated among these units of government? Sometimes
it is said that the role of local governments should
be maximized or that the central government should
undertake only those functions that state and municipal governments cannot carry out. Such statements are a little foolish, for these prescriptions, if
taken literally, would lead to highly inefficient
choices. It is technically feasible to shift spending
authority drastically in either direction. If people
chose to do so, they could put national defense or
the management of the money supply into the
hands of local governments or make the Federal

government responsible for all fire departments. As usual, though, as resources are shifted, the gains from further shifts begin to decline and the costs begin to rise. One should not fasten onto some "requirement" but choose on the basis of judgments about the incremental costs and gains from shifting spending authority from some governmental units to others.

This prescription gives little concrete help, but at least it is not foolish. It gives little help because the costs and gains are very hard to appraise. First, there are no markets to reveal the values that people attach to "another bushel of Federal activity" versus "another bushel of state activity." Thus there are no price tags that have general validity; one can hardly use Pareto optimality as a guide in reaching specific choices; and one cannot use voluntary exchange (at least not systematically) to resolve conflicts in a peaceful and fairly sensible fashion. Shifts of government spending and taxing will involve compulsion and will make some better off and others worse off.

Second, even from any individual's standpoint, the costs and gains from shifts in government spending are extremely difficult to assess, chiefly because such shifts involve complicated interactions with other citizens, vast uncertainties, and pervasive interdependencies. Consider just one illustration of relevant interactions. Would I gain from having the Federal government subsidize municipalities in providing water (good for me if there are no strings attached, and if I live in an area where water is relatively costly to produce) in view of the possible increase in pressures for subsidizing municipal libraries, police departments, and parks (bad for me if I live in an area that would lose more than it would gain and if Federal standardization and control of these activities grew, reducing the future options about such matters that would be open to me and my children)? The relevant interactions are similar to those that cause most people to be concerned about individual rights. One may dislike a particular religion enough to approve of its suppression; what gives one pause, however, is the realization that permitting its suppression might set in motion a chain of events raising the probability of suppressing various other religions and individual rights. Moreover, because of such interactions and for many other reasons, there are great uncertainties about the costs and gains from shifting resources from municipal to other governments (or vice versa). Probability distributions rather than unique estimates characterize the outcomes. Almost nothing is known *with certainty* about the net impacts on oneself, let alone the total impacts. The resulting difficulty of reaching "correct" decisions surely needs no elaboration.

Interdependencies among the actions of various governmental units deserve special mention. They have been stressed in Chapter 2 and elsewhere in this volume. They are the key to many difficulties that beset public spending decisions. Education, law enforcement, sewage disposal, transportation facilities, etc., in Town A often produce real costs or gains to the residents of Town B. Actions of a state government may yield a bewildering variety of costs and gains to citizens of other states and to various local groups. With independent authority, such spillover effects may be serious (consider independent nations, for example). Bargaining among governmental units tempers that independence and leads to better results. Another device, shifting authority to higher levels, puts someone *in a position* to take interdependencies into account, though what he actually does will depend upon bargaining pressures more than upon the goodness of his heart. (However good his heart is, he still has limited energy, time, and other resources, and he presumably wants to survive in government.) How best to coordinate the interdependent actions of different units of government is anything but obvious.[1]

With increasing population, urbanization, communication, and industrialization, these interdependencies become increasingly important. Nations feel growing pressure to find improved arrangements. In the United States, during the 1950s, the Congress set up the Commission on Intergovernmental Relations and later the permanent Advisory Commission on Intergovernmental Relations. The staff of the latter has produced a series of useful studies and continues to examine the more pressing issues.[2] In recent years, the Congress has passed numerous laws and the Supreme Court has reached several decisions that greatly affect our multilevel governmental structure. In its second session alone, the Eighty-eighth Congress provided new grant-in-aid programs to assist states and local governments with outdoor recreation, health facilities, library construction, urban mass transportation, the construction of low-rent housing for domestic farm workers, the improvement of nurses' training, and the implementation of various features of the Economic Opportunity Act of 1964; and there are now more than forty separate programs providing assistance in connection with urban development. Spending by the different levels of government will affect, and be affected by, such crucial issues as the civil-rights struggle and legislative reapportionment. And the evolution of multilevel government may shape the possibilities of world government and the kind of society that ultimately emerges.

---

[1] George J. Stigler, "The Tenable Range of Functions of Local Government," in Edmund S. Phelps (ed.), *Private Wants and Public Needs*, rev. ed., W. W. Norton & Company, Inc., New York, 1965, pp. 167–176.

[2] See the latest annual report of the Advisory Commission and its list of published studies.

disadvantages of having choices made by multiple local authorities

The basic difficulty with having choices made by a multiplicity of local authorities is the interdependence just mentioned. If each community's actions affected only that community, there would be no objection to leaving the decisions strictly to local authorities (just as there would be no objection to leaving each individual's decision completely alone if they brought others no gains or costs). In fact, however, individuals have a stake in the results of certain choices made in other states and communities, and a special district's actions can affect costs and gains to other governmental agencies or municipalities. These interdependencies come about because people move from one place to another—and it matters whether they are diseased or healthy, literate or illiterate, trained or unskilled—and because things and effects (water supplies, air pollution, crime, disease, benefits, tax impacts, and information) move from one place to another.

If local authorities make decisions independently, they neglect the costs and gains to other communities, and produce too much or too little of certain "outputs."[3] As mentioned repeatedly, bargaining among such governmental units, like voluntary exchange among individuals and firms, reduces the neglect of such spillovers. But the institutional obstacles, and the costs of striking bargains among thousands of communities, are formidable; and consequently people keep searching for revised institutional arrangements that might yield more economical (that is, preferred) patterns of behavior. For example, many communities might be willing to pay other cities to provide better health or educational programs; but the holdouts in such imperfect bargaining situations, and the costs of striking comprehensive agreements among numerous communities, often prevent anything from happening. With the present institutional framework, the costs of taking action may outweigh the anticipated gains. As a result, people start considering modified arrangements—Federal grants-in-aid, state control of school systems, perhaps Federal control of certain decisions that were formerly local choices.

Bus and other transport systems in a metropolitan area similarly pose spillover problems that cry out for solutions. If separate communities or private firms act independently, it is often felt that the transit arrangements are not sufficiently coordinated—that interdependencies are not fully taken into account in scheduling buses, reaching investment choices, and so on. It is then argued (often by private bus companies who would like to sell out to the taxpayers at fancy prices) that a metropolitan transit authority should be formed to co-

---

[3] For a systematic examination of the possibilities, see Alan Williams, "The Optimal Provision of Public Goods in a System of Local Government," *Journal of Political Economy*, February, 1966, pp. 18–33.

ordinate these various transport systems. The basic appeal is the same one noted above: people are groping for revised institutions to cope with interdependencies more economically.

It should be repeated, though, that centralization does not necessarily do a better job of taking spillovers into account. As indicated in the preceding chapter, centralization beyond some point reduces the bargaining pressures felt by authorities, makes them less responsive to costs and gains felt by others, and tailors choices to fewer views of the future and fewer utility functions. One tends to think that officials in a position to consider all the spillovers will automatically do so, perhaps because a person visualizes himself handling the difficulty that is plaguing him. But even those officials whose positions enable them to see the whole picture will face specific pressures and have limited capacity to supervise delegated decisions. Thus a Federal education system or a metropolitan transit authority might be less rather than more cognizant of the costs and gains felt by local groups of consumers, laborers, and voters. It is easier for a transportation monopoly to ignore the wishes of specific localities than it is for a system comprising several competing bus lines. To take an extreme example, if certain groups, such as Negroes or residents just outside the city limits, do not get to vote at all, they have little bargaining power in connection with municipal services, and metropolitan transit authorities do not struggle to improve the services to those groups. Most persons can vote, but if they constitute small minorities whose bargaining power is relatively weak, the authorities are relatively unconcerned about costs and gains to those groups.

Another, though corollary, difficulty with multiple local authorities stemming from interdependencies is that individuals and firms will change locations so as to *increase* externalities—that is, so as to avoid costs and reap benefits provided by others. This in turn causes those others to alter their decisions. Thus people move to the suburbs to avoid the taxes yet reap the benefits of the central city, which in turn causes residents of the central city to reduce their health and educational programs, impose payroll taxes, and make other choices according to the costs and benefits *they* feel. Temporarily at least, interdependencies may be still more neglected. Bargaining and the readjustment of decisions will gradually ameliorate the trouble, but people keep moving—and the difficulty does not stand still either.

Another disadvantage of having choices made by multiple local authorities is that it may entail unnecessarily high costs for the performance of particular functions. Certain metropolitan services may be "decreasing-cost outputs." That is, up to a point, it may be possible to produce higher outputs per period at lower unit costs. Tax collection, law enforcement, and sewage disposal are probably good examples. Once again interdependencies (opportunities to internalize some external effects) may be a major factor producing such cost functions. Another factor is that at larger outputs it sometimes becomes economical to introduce an entirely different technology. If there are such "decreasing-cost services," there would be gains from having a central establishment produce them, and these gains would have to be weighed against any costs and disadvantages. Actually, though, surprisingly little is known about the costs entailed by different types of variations in the output of community services.[4]

Another difficulty with home rule, again one that stems partly from interdependencies, is that some communities and states are much poorer than others, and, as it is often expressed, local "needs" sometimes exceed local fiscal "capacity." What does this mean? In my view it means that the poorer jurisdictions can be expected to spend less on the provision of certain services than one thinks they ought to spend. Because they are relatively poor, taxpayers in those areas will choose to spend less than others on school systems, public health programs, and adult training just as they usually spend less on shelter, clothing, and entertainment. One may think they ought to spend more on schools, immunization, and so on because it would benefit others also. Or the reason may be that it seems unfair for people in certain areas to be markedly poorer than people in other areas, yet at the same time one wants them to spend any wealth transfers in particular ways. Or a person may favor subsidizing certain groups because voting arrangements bring these subsidies about, and he regards it as a price worth paying for those voting arrangements.

Nowadays the arguments favoring subsidies are being extended to *all* local governments, and people are concerned about the abilities of such governmental units in general to provide "needed" municipal services. Here one presumably means that local governments are unlikely to spend as much as one thinks they should or that, even if they do spend that much, it is more expensive for local governments to collect the revenue than it would be for the central government to do so. Concerning the latter point, Federal taxation is *relatively* inexpensive for officials to employ, since the central government can use the

---

[4] Stigler, "The Tenable Range of Functions of Local Government." Interesting work has been done on cost functions in this area. See, for example, Harvey E. Brazer, *City Expenditures in the United States,* Occasional Paper 66, National Bureau of Economic Research, New York, 1959; Werner Z. Hirsch, "Expenditure Implications of Metropolitan Growth and Consolidation," *Review of Economics and Statistics,* August, 1959, pp. 232–241, and "Cost Functions of an Urban Government Service: Refuse Collection," *Review of Economics and Statistics,* February, 1965, pp. 87–92; John F. Kain, "Urban Form and the Costs of Urban Services," unpublished paper prepared for the Committee on Urban Expenditures, 1966; and Charles M. Tiebout, "Economies of Scale and Metropolitan Governments," *Review of Economics and Statistics,* November, 1960, pp. 442–444. Nonetheless, the gaps in our knowledge of such cost functions are still enormous.

nationwide progressive income tax. These revenues automatically grow without imposing new decision-making costs on voters, and these taxes seem to have relatively few administrative costs and unneutral effects on resource use. Local taxation is often more expensive than central taxation because of worse impacts on resource allocation, incentives, administrative costs, and votes. The inefficiencies and adverse effects of overlapping taxes have long been recognized. As an example, in taxing cigarettes, "the States are employing an enforcement procedure which is a hundred times costlier than that used by the Federal government to collect about 60 percent as much revenue."[5] One clue to the extent of the difficulty is the fact that there are over 80,000 taxing jurisdictions in the United States. Furthermore, property and other local taxes, apart from high collection costs, tend to be relatively inequitable in failing to treat equals equally and relatively bad in their effects on locational patterns and resource allocation.[6] Thus while local taxes have a major virtue—the support of local autonomy in public-spending decisions—there *are* trade-offs to be considered. The disadvantages of having choices made by multiple local authorities should be weighed against the advantages of doing so; and it is appropriate to consider having state or Federal governments share tax receipts with local units or take over the provision of additional services.

advantages of having choices made by multiple local authorities

Let us now look at the other side of the account: the advantages of leaving choices to a multiplicity of local authorities. This encompasses a whole spectrum of possible arrangements, of course. The discussion will point up some relevant costs and gains from moving toward fewer or more local authorities, but it cannot indicate just where along the spectrum one should stop. Fifty state school districts might constitute excessive centralization, yet the present 30,000 school districts are probably too many. As these arguments for and against having multiple state and local governmental units are reviewed, it will be apparent that many of the points are the same ones presented regarding centralization versus decentralization *within* any governmental unit.

The crucial advantage of home rule on most matters is that it increases the possibilities of catering to local and minority tastes. *Other things being the same*, therefore, minority groups and "nonpreferred persons" might well prefer

---

[5] Advisory Commission on Intergovernmental Relations, *Sixth Annual Report*, Washington, D.C., 1965, p. 23.
[6] For additional information about these issues, see any standard textbook on public finance.

to have functions left with local governments, where they have a better chance of influencing decisions.[7] To Federal administrators, primarily responsible to the majority and the larger minority coalitions, it is costly and not very rewarding to design highly diversified programs. In the production of any government output, there are therefore powerful forces toward standardization rather than a wide range of variations. Consider public housing. Unless strong pressures for variety develop, only a few designs are likely to be used. Housing built by individuals, however, is certain to be more varied. Even low-cost tract developments for sale to individuals turn out in the aggregate to provide more variety than would public housing for the whole community. And public housing controlled by local governments is likely to cater to more taste differences than would public housing controlled in all communities by the Federal government.

Catering to a variety of tastes is important for several reasons. First, it makes possible a better job of satisfying individual preferences, that is, of increasing "welfare" and approaching economic efficiency. To take an extreme case, some can be made better off without making anyone worse off by producing automobiles of several colors, sizes, and designs according to the consumers' preferences rather than one standard automobile. Second, satisfaction can be further increased, because people can vote with their feet;[8] they can move to communities that provide the pattern of services they prefer, just as customers can switch from one brand or store to another. Needless to say, I do not mean that local sovereignty should never be tampered with; especially because of spillovers, one may wish to expose children in *all* communities to certain educational programs or to encourage races to live closer together and try to get used to each other instead of forming ghettos (though one would hardly wish to press *all* subgroups to live near each other in a series of Noah's-ark communities). I am merely pointing out some real benefits of being able to move from one community to another that should be weighed against the disadvantages.

Third, having home rule and catering to local tastes gives a better hedge against uncertainties and mistaken judgments. Education is a particularly important case in point because the costs and gains from alternative programs are highly uncertain. People often believe that experts should identify all our long-run goals, figure out the best educational program to achieve those goals, and

[7] Harold Demsetz, "Minorities in the Marketplace," *North Carolina Law Review*, February, 1965, pp. 295–297. Other things may not always be the same, of course; as a rule, a minority may be able to influence local government at lower cost than it can influence the central authorities. But obviously it is possible to have allies in the central government on certain issues (e.g., the protection of constitutional rights) and to find it extremely difficult to influence local authorities.

[8] This point has been stressed by Charles M. Tiebout, "A Pure Theory of Local Expenditures," *Journal of Political Economy*, October, 1956, pp. 416–424.

provide this program to all pupils having appropriate abilities. Yet the main goal should probably be to provide adaptability, to hedge against uncertainty about goals, future technology, and the future environment in general. The probability is high that the judgment of any one group about the "right" educational program will be a mistake. A multiplicity of judgments is more likely to include good decisions and to preserve or invent valuable features whose value cannot yet be perceived.

A corollary of this point is that home rule provides a hedge, not merely against mistaken judgments, but also against downright vicious officials or majorities. In other words, local sovereignty, and at a higher level states' rights, provide a set of checks and balances that prevents any group from having enormous power. If a group whose views strike me as being vicious gets control of a community or even a state, I can as a last resort vote with my feet. In the end this severely limits the power of the controlling group, and after awhile forces it to restrain itself. Consider the violence apparently condoned by the majority, or at least by the authorities in power, in Mississippi and Alabama during the 1960's. Consider some of the court trials of white persons accused of murdering Negroes or civil rights workers. These events reflect what many would regard as a vicious outcome of majority rule, and an outcome that would probably not occur if murder were a Federal crime. Yet it may at the same time underline the importance of maintaining *many* states' rights. How would one like to have *most* issues decided by one majority ruling, which can sometimes yield this sort of outcome, applying to the entire nation? It would be impossible then to vote with one's feet and hold this particular rein on the power of the governing body. Hedging against such a contingency is an important benefit provided by the dispersal of power among states and local authorities.

Along this same line, it may simply be easier to resolve conflicts if people have the option of moving to a different jurisdiction. Suppose one sees little virtue in satisfying local preferences, hedging against uncertainties or mistaken judgments, or hedging against the emergence of a tyrannical majority. He may still see considerable gain from having multiple local authorities because the option of changing jurisdictions can alleviate conflicts. Of course conflicts can be suppressed by applying enough force, but multiple jurisdictions may reduce the degree of conflict without resort to force.

In a similar vein, the dispersal of authority among multiple governmental units may, by maintaining more options, make the exercise of the basic freedoms less expensive to individuals. As noted in Chapter 7, the more options an individual has, the less costly it is to say what he wishes, worship as he pleases, print what he wants to write, and vote according to his convictions. If his options are reduced, he may find such behavior more expensive from his standpoint, and he demands or takes less of these items. Thus the maintenance of more options by having multiple states, municipalities, and districts may also help preserve basic liberties in this fashion.

Still another hard-to-quantify, yet perhaps extremely important, advantage of having a multiplicity of local governments is the long-run benefit of having citizens deal with local governments rather than just having biennial elections of Federal officials. The long-run prospects of democracy probably depend upon making public spending choices fairly responsive to voters' thoughtful wishes, that is, upon dispersing bargaining power widely. This in turn depends upon the maintenance of an institutional framework that makes it rewarding from the individual's standpoint to acquire information, think about issues, vote, and otherwise participate in the political process. It is all too easy for these activities to be unrewarding from each individual's viewpoint. But the larger his stake and the larger the chance of forming an inexpensive coalition that might affect elections, the greater his incentive to participate thoughtfully in the day-to-day working of the political process. For most of us, these conditions exist in local government to a greater extent than in national government. For these reasons, having a multiplicity of local authorities may keep people participating in the political process, may indirectly increase their interest in (the rewards from) trying to influence national actions. It may even help preserve a feeling of duty to participate in national elections, that is, a tacit agreement that "I'll inform myself and vote if you will."[9]

A final, and more pedestrian, benefit of having choices made by a multiplicity of local authorities is that competition in providing particular services makes for criticism and increased efficiency. Rival bus lines within a metropolitan area; trash collection in each community, or even competing trash collectors within a city, instead of a state trash-collection service provided to municipalities; competition between the public and private schools—all these rivalries, though far from "perfect competition," are better than no rivalry at all in motivating managements to strive for efficiency. The security of knowing you have no competitor is a powerful sedative, and knowing that people can compare your performance with others, even in a rough way, is a powerful stimulant to the quest for better results from available resources. Even for any "decreasing-cost service," the higher costs from having smaller output rates should be weighed against the tendency of competition among government units to increase efficiency.

For instance, many persons feel that purchasing supplies and managing inventories are decreasing-cost activities. To take an extreme example, they might

---

[9] Nations can easily offer rewards or penalties that will induce people to troop to the polls; what may be difficult is inducing them to acquire information about parties, candidates, and issues, and to vote thoughtfully.

urge that a state supply agency buy and store standard items for all communities instead of individual communities having so many small purchasing departments. With modern computers, the inventories could be catalogued, held in a few appropriate locations, accounted for accurately, and managed much more efficiently. There may be something to this. Purchasing officials in each community may find it rewarding to shop somewhat carelessly and to overstock. Yet giving a state supply agency a monopoly of these activities would also bring costs. With only one central agency doing the buying, no one would be able to ask: "Why is Town A paying twice as much for carbon paper or fire hoses as Town B?" With the reduction in competition, would the central purchasing authorities find it rewarding to shop carefully and handle inventories efficiently?

directions to explore

There are of course many possible ways to distribute spending authority among the states, the Federal government, counties, cities, and special districts. Each organizational change or reapportionment, each grant-in-aid, and each string attached to a grant affects the bargaining mechanism and the considerations discussed above. Even from an individual's standpoint, the best arrangement is rarely obvious. The existence of "waste" in an engineering sense does not show that eliminating it would be better. One may be willing to pay a high price, in the form of various imperfections and disadvantages, to disperse power rather widely among levels of government and among units at the same level. Obviously, one can keep hoping to make improvements in the existing situation. Today there may well be too many special districts, about which one hears so many complaints; or perhaps these districts are so independent that they do not have to bargain enough with other governmental units. Some consolidation may be very much in order. But one should struggle to keep in mind the virtues of an untidy fragmented governmental structure and avoid moving too rapidly or too far in the direction of centralization.

Two other factors in intergovernmental relations that merit a great deal of attention are grants-in-aid and tax sharing. It may be possible to devise modified forms that will do less to undermine local autonomy.[10] Again, however, one should struggle to keep in mind the hazards. So far it appears that if Congress draws up highly specific constraints and rules so that Federal officials have little discretion, everyone loses flexibility and in the end local authorities are beholden to Congress anyway. If Congress leaves Federal administrators a good

---

[10] For example, see the discussion of "instant tax credits" by Harold M. Somers in "The Heller Plan: A Critique and An Alternative," MR-67, Institute of Government and Public Affairs, UCLA, November, 1965.

deal of discretion, local autonomy is almost certain to be undermined. To some extent the spending decisions will be made so as to buy convenience, security, votes, and other such items in political officials' utility functions. Even more important, conscientious Federal officials who are responsible for these fund-allocation decisions cannot make random choices. They must do what they think is best for "the nation" or what they think Congress "really wants" or something like that; and to do this they must make it relatively expensive for local authorities to exercise their own preferences.

It might be noted that the Federal government's actions in recent years are exerting rather dramatic influences on the multilevel structure of government. In many of the urban development programs, Federal officials find it difficult or inconvenient to work through established local units, so the proliferation of special districts is encouraged (indeed sometimes required).[11] State and other restrictions on the borrowing and taxing authority of local governments stimulate the establishment of other special-purpose units to evade the restrictions. Now the generation of more special districts may seem like a further dispersal or fragmentation of power, but in fact these special-purpose units are often relatively independent of other local authorities but dependent upon the Federal government. They must reckon mainly with Federal agencies but need not bargain much with local officials. In other words, they are somewhat like agents or extensions of the central government. This has given rise to conflicts and bargaining between municipalities and the Federal government, of course, but it is fairly clear who finds stubbornness more costly and who is winning thus far.

Other Federal programs are also seriously affecting the checks and balances among the several levels of government. The highway program provides an irresistible bribe to local authorities, inducing them to displace thousands of families and businesses, perhaps to embark on public-housing programs to accommodate those displaced, and to become more dependent upon the Federal government. Perhaps states and local units would eventually elect to build these freeways and highways anyway—but in the meantime the relationships between local and Federal governments are changing markedly. A still greater influence will probably be the implementation of the Economic Opportunity Act of 1964. Programs under this act involve *direct* Federal-local relationships (sometimes subject to the veto of the state governor). A great deal of money is at stake, and the result is again to make the independence of state and local

---

[11] For a detailed treatment of these matters, see The Advisory Commission on Intergovernmental Relations, *Impact of Federal Urban Development Programs on Local Government Organization and Planning*, Senate Committee on Government Relations, 88th Cong., 2d Sess., 1964.

governments very expensive to them. In exploring and assessing these various ways of modifying the multilevel structure of government, one should keep these drawbacks in mind.

There are other ways of altering the framework that deserve attention. It may be possible to develop more economical contractual arrangements to take care of interdependencies by voluntary bargaining. The Advisory Commission on Intergovernmental Relations urges joint participation, that is, bargaining, by local units whose development plans or other actions affect each other. The central provision of certain services, such as water supply and sewage disposal, is frequently accomplished by special metropolitan districts nowadays, with various communities in the area contracting for the services. Any economies of scale or interrelationships in production can thus be taken into account. These districts are not dependent upon the central government but are run almost as private businesses.

Indeed new types of private ventures are becoming economical because of the possibilities of internalizing externalities that have grown to be important. As is well known, it seldom pays for one landlord to maintain or improve his property if the entire neighborhood is deteriorating. But a group of owners may find it profitable to contract with each other to redevelop their properties, or more frequently private interests may buy and redevelop large areas. Still more often it is turning out to be economical to develop *new* lands in this way, shopping centers being perhaps the best example. Although there are many variants in contractual arrangements, these centers are somewhat like private communities, with lessees contracting for certain centrally provided and co-ordinated services, such as parking and advertising. Many extensions of these developments may prove to be economical, increasing the degree to which interdependencies are taken into account without impairing local autonomy. It may even be possible to make advantageous use of privately owned and operated communities, if appropriate constraints are devised.

These issues pertaining to the allocation of spending authority, which really amounts to decision-making authority in general, among levels and units of government are crucial ones. Choices here will play key roles in determining not merely whether the nation gets an extra 10 percent of GNP from its resources but probably the degrees of freedom and peaceful conflict resolution that individuals enjoy. Indeed, the skill that is acquired in shaping multilevel governments may ultimately be tremendously important in international relations. Choices about the multilevel structure of world-government proposals may be decisive in determining whether later generations have thermonuclear wars, world dictatorships, or peace coupled with considerable individual freedom.

index

Chile, central government expenditures of, 5
Consumers, 21, 35, 37, 45, 103–105, 114, 124
  in Keynesian economics, 85–86
  of public goods, 68–74, 76
  sovereignty of, 109–111
Cost-benefit (cost-gain) analysis (T-accounts), 42, 73, 127–129, 132–145
  five elements of, 136–140
  individual, 13–19, 57–59, 114
  in program budgets, 132–134
  value engineering as, 156–157
Costs, 34–37, 41, 78, 91, 100, 146–153
  adjustment, 80–85, 92, 105
  bargaining and, 19–21, 24–25
  budgeted, 129–134
  divergence between gains and, 25–29
  of freedom, 113–121
  incentive-fee contracts and, 158–159
  of increased centralization, 147–153
  information, 41, 59–60, 80–85, 92, 98, 134
  multilevel spending and, 162–171
  of public goods, 68–74
  of stock and industrial fund use, 156
  of transfers, 50, 54–55, 57
  (See also Cost-benefit analysis; Externalities; MIC; MTC)
Currency, retirement of, 88

Debt, 93–97
  held by Federal Reserve banks, 94–96
  held by general public, 96
  interest on, 8
  stabilization and, 96–97
Defense spending, 4, 7, 52, 75, 77, 110, 149, 161
  budgeted, 32, 134–135
  deterrent, 70–71
Deficit financing, 88–89, 93, 100
Deflation, 100
  cause of, 80
  measures to combat, 88–89, 91–93, 96–97, 111
"De-goldplating," 156–158
Demand, 37, 98, 103, 124
  aggregate, 81–86, 89
  law of, 17–18, 113

Discretionary authority, 95–96, 101, 171–172
  versus, rules, 89–91
Duplication, 130

Economic Opportunity Act of 1964, 163, 172
Education, spending for, 4, 29, 72, 74, 110, 111, 116, 133, 151–152
  analysis of, 143
  capital-forming, 100
  by central governments, 7–8
  multilevel, 164–166, 168–169
  through subsidies, 75–76
Efficiency, 32–45, 81, 91, 168
  general principles of, 44–45
  methods of increasing, 127–145
   conventional budgeting, 129–131
   cost-benefit analysis, 135–145
   program budgeting, 131–135
  Paretian criterion of, 33–41, 45, 72–75
Equal-pay laws, 61, 122
Equilibrium conditions, 86–87, 89
  budgetary, 93, 101
  identities versus, 102–106
Exchange, interaction as, 20
  voluntary, 19, 23–24, 33, 34, 37, 39–40, 111
Expenditures, government (see Increases in expenditures)
Externalities (spillovers), 25–30, 42, 76
  defined, 25
  divergence in cost and gain of, 25–29
  internalization of, 35, 64–67, 165–166
  from multilevel spending, 163–166, 168
  public goods yield, 67, 69–70, 76

Federal Reserve banks, 94–97, 100
Fiat money, 95
First (second) best, theory of, 35–37, 41–43
Fluctuations, economic, 79–101
  budgetary tools and, 98–100
  causes of, 80, 85–87
  prophylaxis for, 88–89, 91–93, 96–97
France, 5–6, 59